Management Consulting Skills Mastery

Adil Khan

Published by Adil Khan, 2023.

Table of Contents

Copyright 1

About.. 2

Welcome 3

What You Should Know Before Reading This Book 5

This Is What Being A Management Consultant Actually Means 6

Pick The Right Types Of Consulting Firms To Work 9

Reasons To Learn Or Work In Management Consulting 17

Management Consulting Career Path And Skills.................... 20

A Peek Inside The Life Of A Consultant................................ 23

What Do Management Consultants Like Mckinsey Actually Do 29

Consulting Process | How To Become A Management Consultant 35

Understand The Recruiting Process.................................... 39

Recruiting Timeline 45

Resume Tips From McKinsey 47

Additional Resources To Understand Consulting Industry .. 49

Understand Consulting Cases 51

Why Do Consulting Firms Give Case Interviews 52

Case Interview Process 53

Types Of Management Consulting Cases 55

Case Types 57

Understand Business Cases 59

What Is A Decision Tree And How To Use It 60

Why To Create Hypotheses With Decision Tree 66

McKinsey vs. BCG Case 71

How To Succeed In Case Interviews 76

Next Steps 78

How To Become A Great Management Consultant 79

Logistics and Ocean Shipping in Supply Chain Management 85

Introduction 87

The Various Types of Expediting and when do you use each. 89

The Desk Expediting 90

The Field Expediting 91

The Resident Expediting 92

Third Party Expediting 93

Low Risks / Low Value Items 94

High Risk/ High Value Items 95

The Complete Flow Chart of Expediting 97

Basic: Choose The Right Supplier 98

The Order / Contract Acknowledgement 99

Have a Kick Off Meeting - KOM 100

Why You Need A Expediting Report 102

The Types Of Expediting Reports 104

Case of a Minor Delay Reported 106

Case of a Major Delay Reported 108

Make Sure To Have A Final Inspection Done 110

The Shipping Release Note 112

How to Optimize Transportation Costs 114

Coordinate Closely With Your Appointed Freight
Forwarder 115

Support Finance Whenever Required & Certify Invoices The
Payment 116

Have a PO Close Out Done 117

Have Contract In Place For Customs Clearance &
Shipping 119

Clubb Shipments From Same Suppliers If Possible If No
Urgency 120

Clubb Shipments If Same Country/ City 121

Below 50 Kg Always Courier Services 122

Between 50 & 100 Either Courier / Air Freight / Road Freight 123

Above 100 Kg Always Sea Freight Or Road Freight Under Specific 124

Always Coordinate In A Single Mail With Freight Forwarder- Supplier - End 125

Use A Srn For Tracking, Decision Of Mode Of Shipment And To Avoid 126

Certified Lean Management Professional 127

Who this Book is for 128

Welcome to the Mind-Blowing Book on Lean Six Sigma 129

Introduction 132

Five Enablers with Lean Six Sigma for Organizations 136

A special note on SPQP Prediction 139

More About Lean Six Sigma and how it is an Evolution 143

Five Core Skills with Lean Six Sigma 150

Customer Service to Customer Relationship Management 156

Introduction 157

What It Is And What It Isn't 160

Why It's So Important And How So Many Businesses Get It Wrong...163

The 7 Key Ingredients Of Maximizing Your Customer Relationships..169

Introducing The MCR Model 173

How Do Your Relationships 'Measure Up'?.........................176

Review And Refocus Your Approach To Customers.............178

Developing Your Plan 189

Do You Really Know Your Customers?................................190

How To Get To Know Them: Some Simple Steps 197

Establish Ties That Bind 202

Get Personal...204

Create Dialogue Not Diatribes..210

Educate Your Customers And Add Value 219

Maximize Opportunities: Your Options 223

Getting Them To Spend More 224

Customers As An Extra Resource 229

Maximizing Your Customer Relationships: Develop Your Plan 233

Your Next Steps 236

Copyright

About

Management consulting involves identifying and suggesting important changes to what a company does and how they do it—developing a working strategic plan and guiding its execution with optimum effectiveness.

You can see why management consulting is a growing field very much in demand in today's marketplace.

College graduates with management consulting degrees receive offers from top firms with compensation approaching or exceeding $90,000 in their first year alone. Experienced management consultants can earn well over 6 figures—and that's not accounting for bonuses.

Our goal in this training program is to help you improve your day to day operations, career and yourself, so I will show you techniques and toolkits that we use in the management consulting industry, and ones that I frequently share with my clients and students.

You simply have to find a way to acquire practical skills that will give you an edge over the other candidates.

Welcome

The ability to solve complex business problems is a crucial area that affects your career and your personal life. Individuals need to understand how this process works in a context rich and realistic scenario making business decisions and everyday choices ranging from buying a house to designing a sales pitch all relate to problem solving.

Whatever your job or role is, understanding how management consultants solve a business problem can help you make you more successful and prosperous. I'm a professor of business school and MBB consultant and a frequent advisor on company strategy for executives. We're aiming high and we want to teach this ambitious Book, which is a combination of business cases, estimation and brainstorming.

If you get those three core modules right, better position, better compensation and a better life will come to you. In the first part of the Book, I'll be discussing seven types of exclusive case study which could possibly cover all areas of the business world, no matter which industry and line of business you're working in, no matter which phase of your career you've just gone through, you'll always find immensely valuable frameworks, theories, and toolkits that could be fully aligned with your business activities and immediately applied into your work life. Then you'll learn how to brainstorm.

If you do this right, you'll be on your way to becoming the most creative and sharper business consultant. And finally, we'll teach you how to estimate the value in a wide range of businesses with an easy to follow framework. If you're ready to dive in and learn how to use management consulting skills to give you a more successful career, then please join me right here.

What You Should Know Before Reading This Book

Here's what you should know before taking this Book, you should have already at least heard about management consulting. Also, you should have a background in general business. However, you don't need a heavy background in these areas. This is not so much a Book on complex analysis and calculations per se, but Of course that shows you how to develop rigorous frameworks to make our deliverable a completed creative and solid business solution.

This Book is for everyone who is either charged with creating, collaborating or manifesting a company strategy. All great business strategies start with understanding what a critical issue is and how to identify the most crucial levers to achieve a certain business goal. Then going ahead and creating a hypothesis to generate possible options. And this Book is not for experienced strategists. It's a foundational Book designed to give those who are often tasked with executing on a business strategy the tools they need to understand the context of what they're creating.

If you're someone who is looking to shine a light on why people think and feel a certain way about business strategy, this Book is for you. This Book is also for someone who's looking for a consulting position. You'll learn the method to succeed in a case interview. You'll find the most realistic cases and learn how to structure the case that can bring results.

This Is What Being A Management Consultant Actually Means

Consultants. They notoriously charge a lot of money. They travel all the time to the client's site. But what is it they actually do? According to the Oxford English Dictionary, a consultant, a person who provides expert advice professionally. Now, that's a very broad definition, and it doesn't tell us much about what a consultant does in the context we're looking at. Consulting is basically just helping business leaders make decisions around how to run their business, which is super broad, but also a fair representation of what consulting is.

Because depending on the case you're working on, the project can be very different because the problems you're solving are obviously very different in nature at different companies. So what kind of problems do you help them solve and what kind of projects are they? Usually it's a whole range of different projects, so you might have some of the projects I've worked on. One was like turning around an entire business model for a company. They saw their sales were declining. So we came in and we figured out how to change that with obvious things like sales increasing or decreasing a certain metric is like a very simple issue. But then after you dive into that and we ended up changing their business model to drive more revenue, it's just one example of business model transformation.

I've also worked in a private equity group with clients, and so we help private equity firms decide whether or not to invest in certain companies. And that's a very different line of work.

And another project I've worked on was helping two companies merge and figuring out if you could have one company with this set of processes and this company with another, how do you merge them? How do you make the most efficient business when you add the two together? So those are some of the things I've worked on, but there have been very different lines of work. They're all super interesting. Consulting with that definition could apply to someone in law or in medicine, marketing, politics, anything really.

If we're talking about business consultants, then that generally refers to three different types of consulting. First, you have strategy, generally a focus on finance and increasing a company's revenue. Some of the things they might work with their clients on are global expansion or mergers or acquisitions. Then there are management consultants who look at operations and make things more efficient. So it could be streamlining a supply chain or changing the organizational structure of a company. And thirdly, there's technology or IT consulting. And Of course this has to do with technology. So they might implement IT systems or design a specific app for a company.

Consultants don't necessarily have to fit into one of these three categories. These are just the most common ones. And there might also be an overlap between two or more of these categories, whether in an individual consultant role or at an organization overall. So here's our initial overview of what consulting is. Now let's look a little more specifically at what consultants do. Consultants will first be presented with some sort of problem. So maybe the company they're working with is trying to figure out if they should expand into Asia or a different company having communication issues between leadership and management.

The first thing they do is conduct some research. So that could be qualitative research or doing interviews with people at the organization. Or it might be quantitative research collecting data from the client or from third party market research reports, things like that. And using that research, they can either come up with a strategy to present to the client or a solution that could help them with that problem. Typically, the strategy or plan would come in the form of a PowerPoint deck. That's the traditional consultant deliverable. And what happens after the strategy or plan is presented to the client might differ.

Some consultancies just help with the formulation of the strategy. Others might help with the implementation of that strategy or plan, or they might help with both. I know the explanations in this chapter are still quite general, not very specific, but that's because consulting spans so many different kinds of industries. So the clients and the projects that you would work on would be very different from each other. But I hope this chapter is still helpful and it gives you a little bit more insight into what consulting is.

Pick The Right Types Of Consulting Firms To Work

So then there are six main categories of management consulting. They are strategy, I.T., accounting, boutique, internal and independent. There are, Of course, other categories which may be considered, but most management consultants will fit into one of these six categories. So firstly, strategy consulting. Then I'm going to go through all six categories in detail. But let's start here. Strategy Consulting. Well, this is the type of management consultants that receive the most attention.

Strategy Consultants support and advise senior management in a wide range of sectors. They tackle broad questions which relate to the overall direction of a business. The most famous of strategy consultant firms that I can think of include McKinsey and Company, Boston Consulting Group and Bain and Company. Staff at these firms are normally taken from top undergraduate universities and business schools. This helps support the idea that they are the best of the best with the best minds, Of course. Then comes serious pricing for access to their insights. For a team of five, working for a month is often more than $500,000.

Given the scope of the problems they're dealing with, however, this is actually relatively small money for a major company. The type of questions they might look to, things like our competition are becoming more competitive. How do we adapt to defend ourselves? We need to streamline our manufacturing. So which factories should we close? How can we improve our net profit margin? What's the best way to increase our market share? Which market should we launch a new product in? A standard resume at a strategy consulting firm would include experience, such as developing a redesign of a Fortune 500 companies planning function by working with the client's VP's to develop scenarios to stress test the new function.

Subsequently, the client has had million dollar annual savings when joining a strategy consulting firm. An aspect which new consultants enjoy is the wide variety of business questions they are challenged with. This enables them to get a good overview of what happens in business. After 2 to 5 years of work experience, many consultants leave the strategy consultant firms to pursue a career in a specific industry. At this stage of the interview, though, candidates must face case interview questions. In this type of interview, a candidate talks through a business problem with the interviewer. So a typical case may go like this.

Our client is a $1 billion tech company. Recent sales have slowed in their home market and they want to expand into new countries. They need you to identify which market offers the best addressable market for them. Okay, now to consider accounting firms. All of the major audit firms offer consulting work to their clients. The largest firms include KPMG, PricewaterhouseCoopers, or also known as PwC, Ernst and Young and Deloitte Touche, Tohmatsu. All these firms, like strategy consulting firms, look to recruit sharp minds, Of course, but they do recruit from a wider range of universities and strategy firms.

The similarities between accounting and consulting can be really large in number. For example, both types of firms work with senior management at clients. Both need all of their employees to be familiar with business mathematics. The conflict of interest potential at accounting firms is really large. After the Enron and Arthur Andersen scandal in the early 2000s, new legislation was put in place to provide clear rules about how the audit and consulting chapter of these firms can operate. The most famous piece of this legislation is called Sarbanes-Oxley. The question is: can accounting firms deal with what?

Financial tracking and reporting processes are inefficient. How can we improve our compliance rates? How might we improve cash flow by optimizing our billing or payment processes and policies? Whilst you might have noticed that those three questions do seem to be related to accounting, these firms have considerable expertise to deal with other areas, to use just one example. Deloitte's Human Capital Advisory Practice deals primarily with questions about how to deal with human resources and change management. This type of work leads those who work at accounting firms to have experiences that involve, for example, carrying out extensive review of the invoice to cash cycle to identify bottlenecks which slow payments.

Subsequently, the client has seen receivable metrics improve by 28%. During an interview for these firms, they are likely to focus more on behavioral questions and may, but not always quiz your accounting knowledge. Okay. From accounting firms, let's turn now to I.T. specialists. It. Consulting is, Of course, an enormous market. The major firms in this space include Accenture, IBM, Hitachi Consulting, Computer Sciences Corp, CGI Group, and Igate Patni. It's worth noting at this point that, as I mentioned before, consulting firms don't always fit neatly into one category. So for example, Accenture, whilst mainly it does also have a strategy consulting arm. IBM is estimated to have 100,000 IT consultants, but Of course it also makes money and other non consulting business divisions. So IT consulting firms recruit really broadly.

Areas they can focus on include a particular type of coding knowledge, high GPA and rank within your class. Their clients are normally the CTO of a corporation, and the questions they get asked to solve are things like how can we automate this antiquated paper system to how should we go about fine tuning and articulating our specific requirements to receive bids from different It vendors to how should we go about implementing a company wide ERP that's enterprise resource planning software system or CRM, which is customer relationship management system. Examples of such platforms include SAP, Oracle or Salesforce.

Another question might be what new systems should we update our old green screens to? Or how can we ensure our important data is encrypted, backed up, accessible and secure? A normal IT consultant's resume would typically include something like an accelerated online sales process by selecting, changing and testing a CRM solution which streamlined processes which led to shipping times improving by 25%. The standard IT Consulting interview might ask the candidate to explain the process they would use to implement an IT upgrade. Okay. At this point, we've covered the major types of consulting firms which involve the larger names most of you have probably heard of. And I'll now look at the other three types, some smaller others hard to see, but all definitely having their role. All right.

Next is boutique consulting firms. So the boutique consulting firm category really does involve every type of consulting. These firms tend to specialize in a specific industry or practice area, and sometimes in both. There are countless ways boutique firms can specialize. I'll give you one example. ZS Associates is super at sales and marketing consulting to pharmaceutical companies Hewitt, Mercer, Towers, Watson and the Hay Group Focus on HR challenges within HR. Some boutique firms specialize further by dealing with just issues like compensation and benefits. And Marxian associates are two firms which operate in innovation consulting. I think you are beginning to get the picture that the list of what boutique firms can do is pretty much endless.

What you must do, though, is not let the word boutique fool you. Many of these firms actually have thousands of employees and are global in scale. But Of course, many are small and focused with these firms. There are no set rules for how they recruit, and the quality of the firms themselves varies a lot. Now internal consultants for a lot of management consultants, they only have one client and that's their employer. These are internal consultants. It's become common for corporations to have a consulting team which tackles opportunities within the company. Sometimes called a company's strategy group, they are, in effect, a consulting team operating internally. One of the benefits of having an internal consulting team.

The major benefit is that internal consultants already know the business and not insignificant benefit is that they typically cost a lot less than external consultants. And for the employee who is the consultant, they can often advance into key leadership roles inside a company. A lot of large corporations battle with top strategy management consulting firms for talent. They want to recruit the best undergraduate talent onto their internal consulting or rotational programs, depending on the sector. The corporation works on questions which internal consultants tackle.

How can we disseminate our best practices through the company? Which businesses are suitable acquisition targets? What is our competition doing in X country, which we aren't? And Of course, what would our strategy be if a union organized a strike at one of our factories? While the range of questions can Of course be broad for some internal consultants, they focus on just one area. Employees who operate in an internal consulting team are frequently hired from consulting firms. A popular thing for headhunters to do is to try to call management consultants at strategy consulting firms to tell them about opportunities for strategy development in different corporations.

An internal consultant resume would normally aim to highlight a large number of projects they worked on, which then led to saving or generating large sums of money for their employer. Okay. Finally, independent consultants. As the name indicates, they are independent. They do anything and everything. These consultants do not operate under a major company. These entrepreneurial consultants normally work by themselves or in a small team of no more than six. The typical independent consultant will have spent years gaining a deep expertise about a specific business challenge. Who are these people? In some cases, they're semi-retired. They want to keep getting involved in new projects or in other cases, they're new parents who've decided they want to reduce workload.

And sometimes it's a younger person wanting more freedom and flexibility. Independent consultants often supplement their incomes with other work, which may include executive coaching, speaking engagements or other one off projects. These are, Of course, broad categorizations, about six types of consultants, but they are ones which can provide a useful starting point when exploring management, consulting, career options. Which one of these is best? Well, this highly depends upon your background and what your goals are. If you're a hard worker with nothing but top grades in your academic life and you want to become a Fortune 500 CEO one day, aim for a strategy management consulting firm. If you're working towards a CPA.

Accounting firms will value this type of qualification most. If you love computers, coding and process improvement and everything that goes with that, then consulting may give you the best environment to grow. If you have a specific area of knowledge that you'd like to develop every day, then find a boutique firm which specializes in that. If long term stability is a primary goal, then working for an established corporation as an internal management consultant may be the best fit for you.

Reasons To Learn Or Work In Management Consulting

When first starting out in management consulting, your pay is likely to be about $90,000 per annum. On top of that, there are great perks like being sponsored to do an MBA paid time off for you to support a charity and Of course excellent maternity benefits. When you're asked by a recruiter, why do you want to become a consultant? Of course, none of these reasons are what you should say. Your reasons to become a consultant must be more thoughtful and you need to be able to articulate them clearly.

I'll talk you through seven strong reasons for why you might want to become a management consultancy. So to start, I'd like to quote Adam Lapthorne, an analyst at Frontier Economics. One day you could be looking at issues around the uptake of messaging services. The next looking at the effect electrical infrastructure has on house prices in Cornwall. This highlights a main reason that people decide to go into management consulting. The huge variety of projects which are available, the range of colleagues you'll work with and the different types of clients you'll meet.

On top of this, many consultancies also offer international travel opportunities, which provides further varieties. Second one is top notch workmates. I touched on this one in Variety, but it's worth considering this in its own right. The consulting sector attracts top quality graduates, which means you'll be working alongside a pool of diverse and intelligent colleagues who thrive on mixing creative and innovative thinking with a practical approach to how to solve problems. Let me now quote an associate at the Boston Consulting Group. Part of me expected it to be full of stereotypical city job banker types, but everyone here cares about people as well as the work they do. This. That leads me to early responsibility because management consulting firms deal with senior management clients.

This gives you early in your career access to senior people who present development opportunities you wouldn't typically get until later in your career. You'll be given responsibility to work and advise senior clients really early on. Okay. This presents challenges, but hopefully if you're applying to enter this world, then the type of challenges you thrive on. Continuous learning is the next one. Management consulting, Of course, offers the chance to keep learning and developing throughout your career. This builds the fact that you get responsibility early.

You must learn quickly, but given the business environment constantly evolves, you must always learn and improve. And this will help you develop my fifth point, which is an impressive skill set. Philip Decrest, an associate of Parthenon II, commented that alongside my analytical and communication skills, I've greatly improved my time management skills. This skill set you develop in the role will open doors to new opportunities later on in your career. Achieving results, then it's very satisfying to see a development that I've carried out go live and to see the impact it can have on an international finance company, says Jamie Gillespie, a consultant at CHP Consulting.

As a management consultant, you'll work hard. Sure, the hours will be long and the projects will be extremely intensive for weeks, if not months. When you reach the finishing line, though, there is an immense satisfaction from seeing how your work benefits the client. And finally, all degrees sought. Although strong numeracy skills are needed when you're consulting, it can be an advantage to have a degree in business, economics, science or technology. However, it's not essential. The consulting profession does offer a career for those of you with a relevant postgraduate degree, MBA or industry experience. Now let's turn to what actually happens when you're a management consultant to help you understand. I'm going to talk you through a day in the Life.

Management Consulting Career Path And Skills

Let's say you joined a firm, how does your career progress over time? What I've kind of laid out here is, one entry point is a business analyst. So, if you're an undergrad or you don't have a significant amount of professional work experience, and this really varies, it depends on the individual and specifically what they've done and for whom. But, generally speaking, if you're undergrad, you don't have a whole lot of experience, you would join the firm as a business analyst. And there, what are you required to do?

Well, analytics, modeling, you have to know how to use PowerPoint, Excel, so you're basically a grunt or a grinder as I've laid out there. It usually takes between one and a half to two years for you to reach senior business analyst. Of course, it's just the senior level of BA. Typically, at that point, a lot of senior business analysts will leave the firm to go and do their MBA. Now, this isn't something you have to do, but it's a good opportunity because all the major firms will support you financially to do your MBA, and I know that from a lot of the top firms, a lot of the SBAs are doing their MBA at Ivy league schools like Harvard, Wharton, Kellogg, and INSEAD. So, a fantastic opportunity to launch your career in a different direction academically and have the firm support you financially.

Another entry point is the associate or senior consultant level, this is, sort of, what I would call the MBA entry point. Now, do you need an MBA? No, you absolutely don't. A lot of the major firms, such as McKinsey and BCG, have special advanced degree tracks or advanced degree application streams for people that don't have a business background. You would have to have, now this depends, but I would say at least three to five years of real professional work experience. But if you join as a senior consultant or associate, what are you expected to do? All of the things that an analyst does, but at a more advanced level. In addition to that, you're going to be doing more project management, more team management, and more client management. So, you're expected to take on a more client-oriented role.

You're still going to be doing a lot of the same work that the analysts are doing, but Of course, you're going to be taking on more client responsibilities. But you're still a grinder, so make no mistake about it. Even if you join at the MBA level or advanced level, you're still going to be doing all the grunt work. Now, two to three years beyond associate or senior consultant, you would typically advance to the manager level. Once you fit in as a manager, you are what I call a minder. So, now you're going to be managing more work streams, involving more projects, perhaps you are moving towards subject matter expertise which is really what a lot of folks do if they continue on in the consulting industry.

Now, this really depends in terms of time, but three to five years after you've made the manager, you'll advance to principal. And again, it really depends on the timing from principal to partner, maybe three to five years, you'll advance to partner. Principle and partners, they are typically more focused on subject matter expertise, they are going to be focusing on business development. You can read more on the list there in the chapter.

A Peek Inside The Life Of A Consultant

Let's start with my background. I'm part of a five member team that's a manager of four associates. We're working on an operations turnaround project focusing on personnel. What personnel means in this context is that we're looking into points such as how to reward the best employees, improve the average members of staff, and put in place systems which can, if needed, remove underperformers. Now back to the story. My client's HQ and its main operations are based in the same city, just a few hours flight from New York City.

So let's start the day. 7:15 a.m.. The hotel alarm wakes me up. My smartphone is within arm's reach even earlier. The production team has emailed me the PowerPoint chapters I sent the night before. This means I'll not have to spend an hour or two this morning working on them before the team meeting. 745 I'm getting ready when my smart phone buzzes. My manager says he'll be ten minutes late this morning. Hotel lobby is the usual meeting point and from there we share a taxi to the client. The client sometimes likes to save little bits of money on things like this. I consider going back to sleep until I look at my work shirts.

All of them are wrinkled and my sweaters are at the dry cleaners. Sleep here is not an option. 8:10. My shirt is ironed and my laptop bag is packed. I meet the team in the lobby and we hail a taxi. During the ride, everyone's reading the Financial Times or busily looking at their smartphones. The manager asks the group if we're ready for the client meeting at two, and everybody nods that they are. 845. We arrived at the client headquarters. We don't actually spend most of our time at the client HQ as most of our work is in their satellite office. However, this is the monthly progress checkpoint and it has to be done at HQ. 920. Everyone has settled into our office for the day. It's a nondescript conference room on the top floor.

Everyone's a little anxious, but also energized because the CEO's attendance at today's meeting has just been confirmed. I check my emails. I opened the attachment from the production team. Thankfully, it's almost perfect. The occasional typo or missing footnote. And every now and again a slightly weird alignment. But it could have been worse. And these are really easy fixes. Okay. 1030 All the presentation elements of my part of the presentation or the deck have been corrected. I printed out five copies for the team. The plan is to do a quick review at noon and I let the manager know. 1031 Then I can focus on tackling my inbox. It's piled up from the last few days of focusing on the presentation. The topics are varied. I've got emails from an ex teammate asking me detailed questions about our projects. I've got surveys from our firm's HR department recruiters and various other groups.

It's really hard to keep track of just how many. And Of course then there are random thoughts from friends and from other analysts. Okay. 12:00. The team meeting begins. Our firm's main partner on our team is dialing in. She's stuck in another city for a different client meeting. There's a short confusion as we seem to be on the wrong dial code. And it turns out our team secretary has changed everyone to a new dial code.

But the partner was trying to use the old one. Problem solved. 1230. The three other associates have finished running through their chapters and analyses. Only one tough question from the partners so far, but that's not always the case. My manager has seen our material a thousand times, so no surprises from him. It's now my turn to present my part of the contribution.

I work through the chapters, making sure to highlight the So what's specific anecdotes from the client to support my conclusions. And Of course I leave time for questions. There aren't any. Although the partner has noticed that I missed a source for a particular chart. Really annoying, but Of course I can't always catch everything. By one, the team meeting ends. The partner ends the meetings by telling us the senior client has some questions about the scope of the work we've been doing being too narrow, i.e. they want us to be doing more. So scheduled a late afternoon call with the broader team. This means more of our firm's partners to resolve the issue. This could, Of course, mean an increased workload for me.

By 1: 20, I'm having lunch with the team and we've invited some of the client team from the satellite office. Through the last two months, we've been building strong working relationships with the three member client team, and through socializing, even if forced, we've gotten to know them at least a little bit on a personal level. After the meal, we head back to the office to prepare for the meeting at two. The client meeting starts and I'm going over my chapters in my head. I'm not presenting, but I know that if there are any questions about my chapter, if that's about data or methodology, then I'll be the person called upon to explain.

At 205, the client CEO enters the room. Everyone's attention is immediately focused on her. She smiles, shakes each one of her hands. Her VP and our senior client Lead tells her that we've worked together very closely these last two months and are looking forward to sharing our findings. We're all a bit nervous. By 245, the presentation is in full swing. My manager is taking the CEO through one of my chapters. The CEO has been silent up till now, points at a graph and says, Wow, is this actually the improvement you've seen? We're the first performance numbers consistent across all of our employees. Everyone looks at me. I check I'm looking at the same chapter on my laptop as she's looking at on the projection screen. I then quickly share facts and figures, which at this point I know without doubt comments I made.

Yes, this is an improvement of 150% over the prior year based on a pilot scheme involving 15% of the workforce. The initial performance numbers were not consistent across all employees, but 85% did fall within a plus minus three point range. My manager flashes a smile in my direction. I've done my job. The attention of the room once again returns to the CEO and the meeting continues. And three, the meeting is over. The client CEO seems to be happy with our findings. She mentions to our firm's partner on the phone with whom she's worked a few times before that our partner has yet again found a super team. She says she's looking forward to seeing where we'll be by the end of the project in four weeks. Our manager is really happy with this public praise. 320. We said our farewells.

Our team goes back to the original room for a debrief about the meeting. Upon dialing in, our partner says thank you to all of us and mentions briefly the scope issue discussion call, which will be at four. So the discussion call involves three partners and my team. My manager spends the next hour increasingly frustrated because the partners can't agree on a single point, not even on how to address the scope issue, which member of the client we should address it with and what actually we should be doing as our recommendation. Finally, two of the three partners have to leave the call due to another meeting. The lead partner who we've been working really closely with remains on the call. She tells us she'll try to follow up with the other two partners and get a consensus.

Once the conclusion has been found, she'll let us know the details. So we return to our laptops. 5:40 p.m. A large email attachment from a client team arrives in my inbox. It's the new employee performance data gathered from the latest quarter. They wanted to share the latest with me so it can be input into the model we've built. I look at the data. It's a mess. Very hard to process. The third of the employees are actually missing from the sheet. Data isn't the correct format. Different attributes are combined into one cell. The cleanup is going to take hours, and it's going to need a variety of Excel functions. I plan to work on it later tonight and tomorrow. 610 Then my manager packs up and suggests we go home early. 6 p.m. is early.

The days have been long but successful. Tomorrow has a really busy schedule which is packed with client interviews. We want to improve the qualitative insights to support what we're finding in this data. 625 The whole team gets in a taxi back to the hotel. Three associates are on their phones speaking with their partners. My manager is having a catch up call with our lead partner. I put in my headphones, turn on my music, and mentally plan out my light. It's going to involve the gym, room, service, dinner and several hours spent cleaning and making use of all that data. I was sent earlier and that is where my story ends. As you can see, it's a really full day, but it involves a wide range of skills.

What Do Management Consultants Like Mckinsey Actually Do

So graduates, considering which career to pursue consulting is one of the most appealing. What consulting involves each day, however, isn't very well understood. This is mainly due to the broad scope of work consultants do with other professions. It can be clearer cut for outsiders to understand. If you take corporate bankers, for example, they value companies, lawyers, draft documents, accountants count things. Consultants, on the other hand, solve their clients' problems. Obvious questions which spring from this are which problems and how do they solve them?

Solving problems can mean anything, and for consultants as a sector, it can mean doing anything from increasing the operational efficiency of a French food conglomerate to helping a print magazine monetize its online operations to cutting costs in a global retail bank based in South America. It's therefore safe to say that consultants are not always clearly distinguished from other professionals by the content of the work they do. The best way to think about that is their main difference from other professions is how they approach problems. We're given a problem. Consultants follow a structured thinking approach.

We can break this approach down into five steps. So let's start with understanding the client industry. Since consultants work with a wide range of projects, they frequently need to build from nothing their knowledge of the industry, client and function. And they'll need to do this each time they begin working with a new client. What this means in practice is that consultants have to understand how their client's industry works and what competitive advantages their client has. Once this is understood, they can begin to be able to get into the details of the problem.

For example, if they don't understand how a publisher makes money, it'll be hard to advise them on whether they should sell or keep a magazine title, or it'll be difficult to advise whether or not to put a paywall on a newspaper website to get an overview and understanding of an industry. Consultants use lots of sources: industry reports such as Mintel Keynote, Euromonitor or Verdict retail reports, analyst and brokers, reports on listed companies, company accounts, both their clients and competitors. General press coverage via Factiva searches, such as in the Financial Times or the Wall Street Journal specialist press coverage for their clients' industry, internal knowledge management systems. These are systems which consulting firms have which should have on file past cases from relevant industries and clients.

And finally, colleagues and experts who have worked on similar industries, clients or problems. It's through all of these, not just one signal source that a consultant puts together a detailed picture of what's happening in the industry. Once a consultant feels they have a good overview, the second step is to identify key questions and establish key hypotheses. This goes to the heart of what consultants are tasked with doing. They're there to answer big questions such as How can a newspaper make money from their website? Or How can a regional airline attract more international customers? Such vast questions need to be broken down into more manageable parts, and these parts need to be structured to ensure that all aspects of the problem are dealt with and that the solution is found in the most efficient way.

When scoping your work, the key is to identify the most important questions. This will ensure you and your client are on the same page. This may sound basic, but this beginning helps you to focus efforts and provides a framework for structuring future analyses. It can also be important to establish some quantified hypotheses early on to help shape your approach. Hypotheses can vary widely, but let me give you some ideas. Again, using the newspaper aiming to make money on its website as an example, we could include will earn X million of revenue charging users a subscription fee over Y period with an X million of revenue by offering users additional e-commerce services which are not offered yet on the website, will earn X million of revenue by placing more ads through the website.

Once you have your hypotheses, you should then structure your work to verify them. The structure you put in place aims to ensure that your planned workflow answers the problem exhaustively and efficiently. There are many frameworks used by consultants for structuring their work. The pyramid principle is viewed to be one of the best when using the pyramid principle. Each statement has to support the main conclusion, which is then divided into issues and sub issues. When putting your ideas into the pyramid, there are three principles to remember.

Firstly, an idea at any level of the pyramid must be a summary of the ideas group below them. This ensures the logic of your answer and exhaustiveness of your supporting statements. Secondly, ideas in each grouping must always be the same type of idea. An example would be a grouping focused on revenue or a grouping concerned with the costs of the business. Thirdly, and finally, ideas in each grouping must always be logically ordered. Don't forget that they must always be logically ordered. You can do this by.

Knowledgeable by importance. Doing this ordering ensures that your problem framework will have no overlaps and it will be exhaustive. You must note, though, that all frameworks should be of the right logic and design. It's not the case that one size fits all. For example, consultants won't use an organizational structure as a framework when looking at processes. As I mentioned, there are many frameworks used by consultants to frame and structure a problem. I'll touch on a few more. Value chain Analysis. This involves breaking down an organization so you can establish which parts generate revenue and what value is created in each of these parts.

Financial frameworks. These frameworks, as the name suggests, focus on analyzing the finance of a company. This may include looking at how profit and revenue relate to each other in terms of total quantities and at the per unit level. SWOt Analysis. One of the quickest but most powerful ways to consider an organization's strengths, weaknesses, opportunities and threats. Porter's Five Forces. These are used to model the attractiveness of a specific business or an entire industry. So once you've determined which model or models you will tackle the business with, you should then fourthly, identify tasks and timings. These tasks and the research they involve should align with verifying your hypotheses for each hypothesis.

Consultants normally consider what they need to do to confirm their assumptions. While the steps up to this point may have been done by one consultant, they also may have been done by a small team. If you are working by yourself, then the next step is to agree with your team. The priorities and timings for completion of each chapter of the analysis. Working backwards from key milestones such as a team meeting with the partner involved is a great way of deciding how much time you should combine with the reality of how much time you actually have. Once you're happy with the schedule, make sure the client is happy too. You need to ensure they're happy with the direction and timing of the work that you're doing.

What type of tasks might this involve? A consultant might need to analyze data, for example, in order to confirm an assumption that only a minority of users will be willing to pay for a newspaper's content online. Consultants might conduct a customer survey, analyze additional available information about a competitor, talk to an industry veteran to get their opinion. Now, you've understood the industry and you've explored and tested your hypothesis, so it's time to produce your final report. This is the final step. You'll have performed your analysis and have your results.

What is key here is clearly communicating the team's findings to the client. This is where entry level consultants typically feature most in the workflow of a project. You now have a reasonable idea about what's involved and what type of consultants there are and what the work may involve. So let's take a step back then and look at how to become a management consultant.

Consulting Process

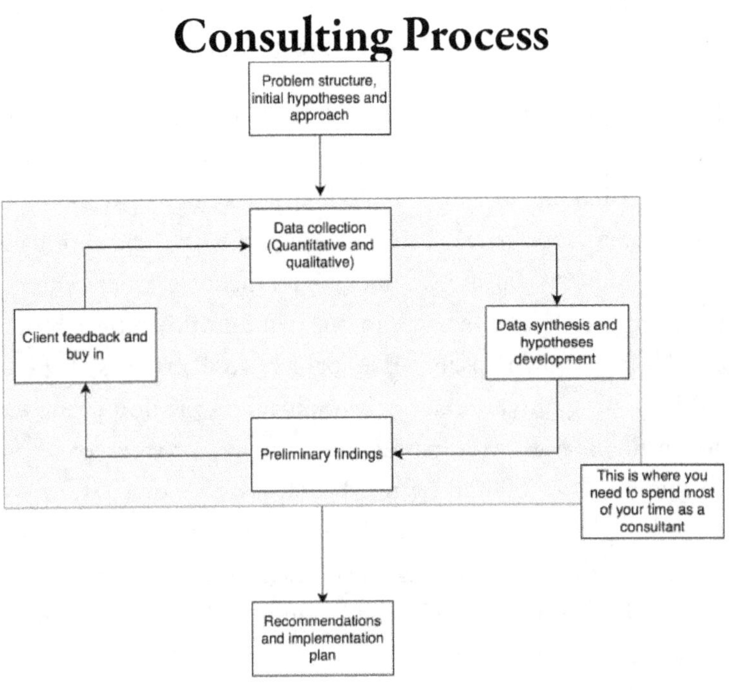

How To Become A Management Consultant

How to become a management consultant. The most obvious route to people is to earn a degree in business administration or a related field. A bachelor's degree is required for most entry level positions in management consulting. However, a bachelor's degree program, which specifically gets designed for business analysts, is rare. This means that many individuals earn their degrees in a related area, such as business, administration, finance, business management or accounting. If a student knows the specific field of consultancy they want to pursue, then they may consider a degree in that specific area.

For example, someone interested in computer systems may wish to earn a minor in computer science. Other Books which are considered helpful include marketing, psychology, government, political science, engineering and human resources. Some businesses and government agencies require candidates to hold a master's in business administration, more commonly known as an MBA or a related master's degree. Business programs are extremely popular. They're now available at most major universities and many private colleges throughout the United States. If you can't or don't want to attend a physical university, there are an increasing number of quality distance learning business degree programs being offered by both well-established traditional institutions and fully online schools.

However, students should always be cautious when looking at these programs. They must make sure and confirm that a program is fully accredited before paying for and beginning their Book of study. So a degree, ideally in a related area, can be useful for opening the door of opportunity of working at a management consulting firm. By itself, however, you're not guaranteed an interview or a job. You should also look to gain high level experience. Work experience is useful regardless of which job you're considering. However, it's crucial in the field of consultancy and management analysis, ideally before or at least immediately after graduation, that aspiring management consultants should pursue an entry level position with the firm they wish to work for. Will you be paid?

Well, there is paid employment for starting positions, particularly in the private sector, but non paying internships as a way to get your foot in the door are also worth considering. Many people become management consultants after years of employment, so fresh graduates may want to consider beginning their careers in a related field. Work experience and on the job training allows for a wider range of employment options as one's career advances. So a good degree and relevant work experience can help you get the job. Some management consultants take it a step further, though, by considering certification.

It's not a requirement to be a management consultant to get any type of certification. Having this, however, can provide the holder with a real advantage over non certified job seekers. There are a number of professional associations and organizations which offer certification. The best recognized certification is certified management consultant. Also known as CMC, which is offered by the Institute of Management Consultants USA. Candidates for the CMC certification must fulfill several requirements. Importantly, this includes three years in practice as a full time consultant. In addition to having a degree from a four year college and the completion of exhaustive written and oral exams.

The Institute of Management Consultants claimed that less than 1% of consultants working today have actually achieved the certified management consultant title. For somebody, however, who's already been working for several years and has a solid professional reputation in their industry, then they might want to consider specialization and independence. What this means is that the individual will start their own firm. Now, this is not for everybody. Being an independent consultant requires a good head for business and a strong entrepreneurial spirit. It will normally involve significant risks. However, if successful, it can be highly rewarding financially and for personal development. Okay, let's move on now to recruiting.

Understand The Recruiting Process

The key components to the recruiting process are company information events. Applying for an Interview by phone. Interview in person. The waiting Period and the Offer. We'll start right at the beginning with company presentations, mixers and information sessions. If you're currently in school, undergraduate, business school or doing a master's, then companies visiting campus will be a common occurrence.

Consulting firms ranging from Boston Consulting Group to Mercer, HR to Kurt Salmon arrive on campuses around the world to give presentations, hold social mixers and other activities, all in an effort to publicize their firm and identify candidates they view as high potential. At these events, there are very few ways to truly beat expectations, but plenty of ways you can make no impact or worse, a negative impact. My key do's for these events are to dress sharply. Aim to meet a minimum of three consultants or people from the company recruiting.

Make sure to ask for their business card post event. Remember to follow up in order to ask for advice and interview tips. What you mustn't do, though, is spend the entire evening talking to your friends. Also, don't spend the entire time by the snack bar enjoying what's probably pretty free food. Don't hand your resume to recruiters or consultants unless specifically asked. Also, while you want to have some questions ready, don't drill your way through 50 of them. They will remember the applicants that they found annoying.

Stage two, the application, the resume, and the cover letter. There are many variations of how this process works. It varies firm by firm. If you're currently studying, there are normally resume submission periods, followed by a selection process which decides who they want to call for an interview. If you're not studying or the firms you want to work at, don't actively recruit at your school. It will normally mean submitting your resume through friends you may have at the firm. Contacting a firm's HR department and via recruiters.

You could also apply in person at career fairs. All of the latter methods are more opaque and so you end up waiting indefinitely to hear back. Whichever method you choose, a very good resume will always make the recruiter look twice. Cover letters, while often essential, present a lot more room for errors and tend not to have much upside. My key do's to make a resume and cover letter and make sure that your resume is consulting ready. So make clear what experience you have that is relevant to the role on your cover letter.

Make sure you have the correct firm and address, etcetera. If you're dealing with a recruiter, make sure to follow up if you don't receive confirmation that they've received your application. Once you've applied, make sure your contacts know that you have applied potentially, then they can then send a positive recommendation to their HR team. What you shouldn't do is send more than one email to ask about the application status. Don't have more than one page for either your resume or cover letter. Don't send additional materials such as a portfolio or a letter of recommendation unless you have been specifically asked to do so. You'll need to narrow your scope at some point, although I do suggest you submit your resume to as many management consulting firms as possible.

If you do receive plenty of interview offers, you should then focus on which firms are the best fit and then prepare most for those ones. So the next step then is an interview by phone. Hopefully, as you will have guessed, these are interviews done over the phone. They normally focus on how you fit into the firm. Now the reasons firms do phone interviews instead of in person can be because of a few reasons. Possibly the firm doesn't have enough resources to immediately hold in-person interviews. It could also be that you're a borderline case and with the phone interview they aim to understand your background better so they can make a more informed choice.

I suggest with phone interviews the focus is the quality of the answers as it's harder to build up a meaningful relationship over the phone with the interviewer. Some consulting firms will have phone interviews and others won't. There are some which skip directly to in person. Others, though, will use several phone interviews before any in-person interview. When during a phone interview. You've got to ensure it's in a quiet area and that your phone's reception is good. Ideally, get on the landline to avoid any drop off of signal. It's okay to ask for time to collect your thoughts, but don't take longer than half a minute.

Make sure you have a pen and paper to hand. They'll be really useful for notes during questions. And if you don't already know the person calling, ask for their email address and follow up with a thank you note. What you should avoid doing is doing the interview while on the move on a train is a definite no no. Don't be too casual because while you may not have the formality of an office surrounding, it's still a job interview. In that same vein, avoid excessive laughing and keep discussion of personal matters to a minimum. Unless, Of course, the interviewer directly asks, okay, we've got the phone interview out of the way. So the next stage then is the in-person interview.

Let's pause for a moment and note that if you've made it here, this is already a great achievement. This shows the firm values what you've already achieved, and now they want to get to know you as an individual. What this means in practice is they want to see your communication skills on the spot, thinking, analytical abilities, your presence and personality. This is the most difficult stage. Other people at the interview will be very well qualified candidates. Stand out from the crowd in a management consulting interview. The key is to do very well on your case question or questions. Have well rehearsed but natural responses to questions you can prepare for.

For example, questions about your CV, you should make sure you're well informed about current business news. If you're looking at a specific industry, know the latest from that industry. It sounds really simple, but it takes a lot of preparation to make this happen smoothly. The best way to think about interviews, both in phone, phone and in person, is that they are having essentially two components. They are the case study and the behavioral questions. The important point to know is that the case study normally accounts for at least 50% of your final score. So it's going to have a big impact on whether you get an offer. Okay. The interview stage is over and you enter the waiting period like the very start of the process when you're getting to know the firm. There are very few ways to improve your chance now of getting the job.

There are plenty of ways, though, to ruin your prospects. You need to be patient. If you have no contact within a week, it may be worth sending a polite email to follow up the recruiter and see any other suitable people in the firm. If you send a daily email asking for an update, no matter how much you want to, you'll damage your chances of them giving you the role. What you should never do is assume you have an offer and stop searching. If you have other interviews coming up, definitely prepare for them. Now, hopefully, having overcome the really nervous waiting period, you will receive the final step, the offer.

This is a big deal. Getting an offer from a top management consulting firm is tough, and it's rare. To give you an idea of the difference in scale, consider that, for example, McKinsey's New York office, one of their largest, occupies between 10 to 15 floors of a single skyscraper. Goldman Sachs, a leading financial firm with a similar reputation of being the gold standard for its industry, has three skyscrapers in New York, all to itself. This is the period when due diligence is done and contract negotiation takes place if any negotiation is needed.

The first thing, though, is to thank them for the offer. Contact everyone in the firm you've spoken to or met to also thank them. Schedule a time to discuss the offer and ask questions of them before going into that call. Try and gather as much information as you can from current and former employees, friends, books, etcetera. Any administrative questions like salary benefits ideally should be dealt with. The HR person who is dealing with you. What you shouldn't do is accept the offer immediately. The exception to that is 100% sure it's the job you want. Don't ask any non HR contacts, any administrative questions unless perhaps you know them well.

Don't start negotiating details of an offer without fully informing yourself first about the company and what exactly it is reasonable to negotiate about. With that in mind, a general rule is don't negotiate anything that won't significantly change your decision about whether you'll take the job or will impact your satisfaction once you're doing the job. So this concludes our walk through the management consulting recruitment process.

As you can see, it's straightforward, but the devil really is in the details and it's not an overnight event. That's why you must practice and understand elements which will be coming up in an interview. So in the next chapter, we're going to look at the case study.

Recruiting Timeline

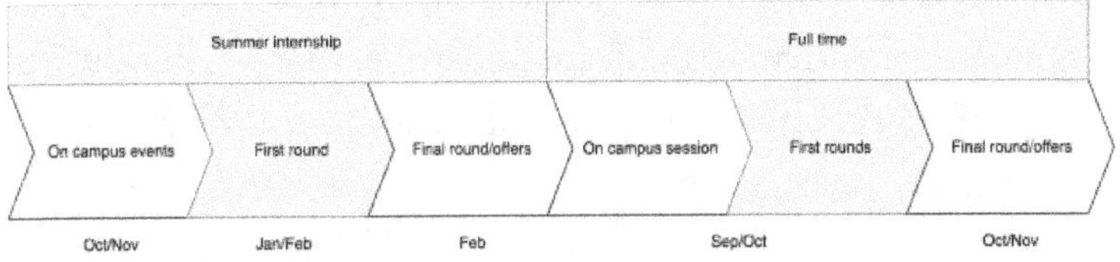

To talk a little bit about the consulting recruiting process specifically, this is a very important point, in terms of what are the good times to be applying for consulting now. Hypothetically, you can apply at any time, you can apply tomorrow, you can apply a week from now, but the best time to apply is when the firms are actually organized and ready to do recruiting. This is something that all the firms follow globally.

Now, I know the timing may be a little bit off, I know that in Europe, it typically is about a month behind where it is in North America, so they are about a month later on they're doing these things but it's very similar. There are two times you need to be considered. So, right now, January, February are when firms are recruiting for summer internships. If you wanted to apply for a summer internship, now's the time you want to be doing it, you may have missed unfortunately some of the application deadlines. But summer internships now are when they are recruiting for it.

Also, if you are interested in full-time opportunities doesn't mean that you can't apply right now, you absolutely can, and it's a good time to apply. Because in consulting, they don't have

HR groups or HR individuals that are doing interviews with candidates. The consultants are the people doing interviews. So, if you imagine and you know that consultants are very busy, it's not easy for them to dedicate time to recruiting. But during the Jan-Feb timeframe, they are dedicating a lot of time to recruiting.

The other time that's extremely critical and important for everyone in the audience is in September and October, so if you want a full-time job in management consulting, September and October are when the firms are going to be heavily recruiting. They're going to be on campuses conducting information sessions, inviting students for first, second interviews, and the whole process kicks off in September. And they are going to be making offers, full-time offers to start in October for the following summer. They are making offers in October and sometimes in November, but candidates won't be starting until almost a year later. So, is this you? Does this work with academics?

Now I know PhDs, they don't necessarily have a firm time that they're going to complete their degree. But something you won't think about as you're recruiting, you may not get brought in right away, there may be a long delay before you start your role with a consulting firm. And the other important things is, again, in terms of the best time to be applying to a consulting firm would be in September and October, because those consultants are dedicating time to recruiting, and there's going to be people in the office that are going to have time to look over applicants resumes and cover letters.

Resume Tips From McKinsey

Resume tips It starts with the resume. We wish we could eliminate the impersonality of the resume review process, but we do believe it is the most equitable way to consider our many applicants. Because your resume, along with all of the supporting information in your application, determines who gets interviewed, it's obviously a critical first step. We encourage you to do the following: · Make sure your resume accurately reflects your achievements and their scale. · Make your resume as specific and non-generic as possible.

A well-crafted resume will also give us a sense of who you are as a person, as reflected in the activities and achievements that matter to you. Key areas for focus We are generally looking for five attributes, which should be highlighted through the examples and supporting details you provide—these include a proven ability and achievement in these traits: · personal impact · problem solving · entrepreneurship · leadership · an overall orientation toward achievement Education In reverse chronology, please include the following: · your university · degree granted and graduation year, including subject of your degree · degree grades, major prizes or awards, significant academic projects, etc., including key dates (e.g., magna cum laude overall; summa cum laude in first year, senior thesis, major research work) · scores for any standardized tests such as the GMAT, LSAT or SAT and transcripts (if required as part of your application) · If you studied in an academic system that may be unfamiliar to us, if possible, please try to explain the results in context; for example, you scored in the top 2 percent of students nationally.

Work experience Beyond your day-to-day responsibilities, we're interested in your achievements and the impact you had based on your direct involvement. Feel free to describe any unique skills, experience, and entrepreneurial successes that you would bring to our culture. Other skills and achievements Your resume should be as complete an autobiographical snapshot as you can reasonably present. Please include any volunteer and charity work or positions of responsibility in professional bodies—especially where they reveal initiative, entrepreneurship, or extraordinary commitment.

Don't overlook the same kind of accomplishments regarding extracurricular activities and significant participation in sports, games, clubs, societies, or hobbies. A high level of achievement in these areas tells us about your commitment and motivation. Languages Include all languages for which you have business conversational ability or better, including an estimation of your level of fluency. Source: http://www.mckinsey.com/careers/join_us/resume_tips

Additional Resources To Understand Consulting Industry

The McKinsey Mind: Understanding and Implementing the Problem-Solving Tools and Management Techniques of the World's Top Strategic Consulting Firm 1st Edition https://www.amazon.com/McKinsey-Mind-Understanding-Implementing-Problem-Solving/dp/0071374299

McKinsey's Marvin Bower: Vision, Leadership, and the Creation of Management Consulting

https://www.amazon.com/McKinseys-Marvin-Bower-Leadership-Management/dp/0471755826

The Mind Of The Strategist: The Art of Japanese Business

https://www.amazon.com/Mind-Strategist-Art-Japanese-Business/dp/0070479046/ref=pd_lpo_sbs_14_t_0?_encoding=UTF8&psc=1&refRID=QME

Websites:

Glassdoor

https://www.glassdoor.com/Reviews/McKinsey-and-Company-Reviews-E2893.htm

Vault

http://www.vault.com/company-rankings/consulting/vault-consulting-50

50

Evisors

<https://www.evisors.com>

Understand Consulting Cases

We'll start with the case study fundamentals. What is a case study? Well, it's an accounting activity event or problem. It'll involve a real or hypothetical situation and aims to include complexities which you'd encounter in the workplace. The goal of a case study is to help explain the complexities of a real life influence on decisions.

When analyzing a case study, you'll have to apply your knowledge and your thinking skills to a real situation. For you to actually learn from a case study, you'll need to be analyzing, applying, knowledge, reasoning and drawing conclusions. Carlos and Smith in 1979 set the following criteria, which a case study needs to meet in order to be considered good. First, it's taken from real life, although it's fine for the two identities to be concealed.

Second, the case study should consist of many parts. Each part will normally end with a problem and have points for discussion. There doesn't need to be a clear cut off point to the situation. Next, the reader must be provided with sufficient information to tackle the problems and issues in the case study. And finally, the case must be believable. To do this, a case should contain the setting personalities, a clear sequence of events, problems and conflicts. Once you have the case presented, we need to do our best to analyze and to solve it.

Why Do Consulting Firms Give Case Interviews

Thinking about why consulting firms give case interviews? Well, I think the first and most important reason why you're given case interviews and what they are looking for is to understand your logical thought process. So, how do you solve a problem? The other thing they are looking for is your testing and your analytical capabilities.

It's not enough to be able to think about how you can structure and approach to solve a problem. You actually have to be able to analyze and assess data and information. So, it's not just math, although you will be doing some mathematical calculations in a case, quite frankly, it's very straightforward, very simple math, multiplication, division, but they are going to test your analytical capabilities.

Thirdly, and perhaps underlying the entire interview process. So, the fit, the case, and candidate questions, they are going to determine your candidates, clients, and project readiness. So, this is almost like an X-Factor. Do you have the confidence that is required to successfully manage a project, to work with a client? I mean, I said that thinking about what is on their mind is they are assessing you from a client perspective, if they are thinking could they staff you on a project as early as tomorrow? And put you in a room with clients, stakeholders and feel confident that you'd be able to manage that situation.

Case Interview Process

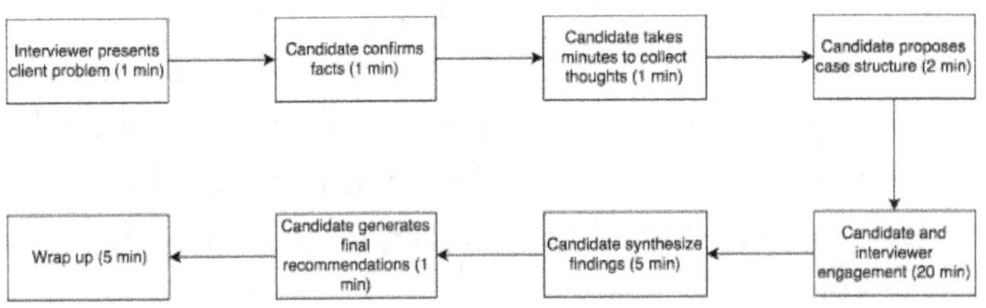

In this chapter, we will focus on what a case interview feels like from a process perspective? Or what sort of steps does it go through? I think this is important to introduce because once you understand what a case is and you start practicing, there are certain rules you'd better follow. The analogy that I use is sort of like the rules of the road, right?

Light turns red, you have to stop; lights turn green, if the sign says don't turn right, you can't turn right, perhaps you can, you'll get a ticket, but the idea is, there are certain rules you need to be aware of in order to drive on the road. Well, there are certain rules you need to be aware of as it relates to case interviews and how they flow. So, just a quick intro here, the way the case is going to work, the interview is going to present you with a problem, typically verbally.

And I say verbally because Monitor, which is now part of Deloitte, they would give the candidate chapters, so you would get a series of chapters, perhaps 10 or 15 PowerPoint chapters, and you'd be required to go through all those chapters, pull chapters out you thought were relevant and answer a question that was posed to you at the beginning of the interview. But typically, you are going to be presented with the problem verbally. The first thing you are going to do is clarify facts. You're going to make sure that you understand the information that was presented to you. Then you are going to actually, literally, say to the interviewer, 'I'm going to go ahead and take a minute to collect my thoughts,' and this is a minute of quiet reflection.

When I say a minute, I don't mean five minutes, I mean 60 to 90 seconds maximum. And this is when you're thinking about how you want to approach the problem. Then you are going to share that approach with the interviewer and ask for feedback to believe you'd say this approach seemed reasonable to you, and they may give you a little bit of feedback about how they feel about your approach. Then the next step is really that collaborative Q&A that I was talking about. So, this is where you're going to be working through the problem with the consultants.

Near the end of the case, it's going to be time to come up with a recommendation, and you are going to take another minute of quiet reflection to come up with that recommendation. So, really, during a case, there are only two times when you're able to be quiet without saying anything. Other than that, you should be thinking out loud and talk to the consultant the entire time. Near the end of the case, when it's time to develop a recommendation, you take another minute of quiet reflection and come up with that recommendation and then you are going to share that recommendation.

Types Of Management Consulting Cases

There are three categories of management consulting case studies in this Book. There are business cases, brainstorming and estimation cases. In the first part of this training program, we'll focus on business cases as those are the primary case types that test what a consulting firm is looking for. A business case allows us to explore a real business situation and a thorough analysis to create a solution to the complex problem.

Examples of business cases include Firm X's profits have been in decline for the past two years. What has caused this and what would you recommend helping Firm X improve its performance? Firm Y makes rings and is considering expansion into the fashion retailing business. Would you recommend it? Firm Z makes tin cans. It's planning to expand its manufacturing capacity and is debating whether to add to its existing plant or build a new one.

What do you recommend that it do? The second category is the estimation case. This type of case can be used in a full business case or separated into analysis in an interview. Examples of estimation cases are estimating the weight of an Airbus A380 estimate. The number of Ford cars in Berlin estimate the number of gallons of blue house paint sold in France over a year. Management consultants are hired to solve the most complex business problems. Therefore, a great consultant needs to be efficient. Creative and sharp.

Brainstorming cases will act as a critical tool, which can greatly boost the chance to generate great business recommendations. Examples of brainstorming are when the government of an Asian country is scared of an outbreak of an aggressive flu strain in a neighboring country. What should they do about it? Or help a local school increase the math scores of its students in standardized tests? This is the overall structure of this Book. So in the next chapter, we'll focus on the business cases.

Case Types

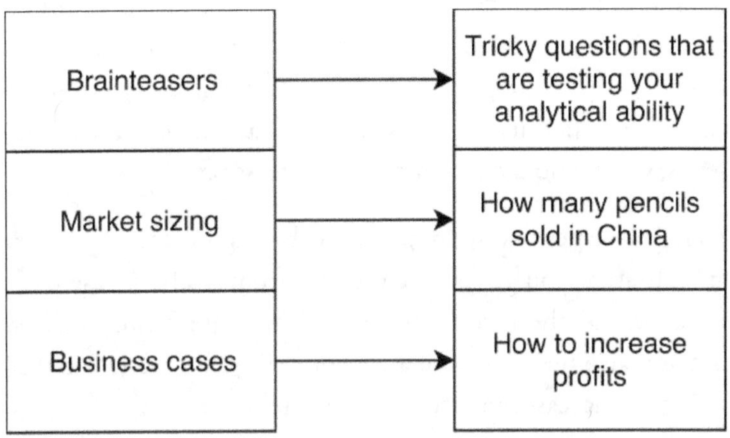

At a high level, there are three case type categories. And a case interview may have components of each. What I've done here is lay them out. The foundation of case interviews is, quite simply, called business cases. The case examples that I provided to you in that chapter are business cases. These are the cases that you are going to get 99% of the time.

But there are also some other sorts of business problems with cases deeply aware of. One is market sizing, and unfortunately, I don't have the time to talk about market sizing in much greater detail. Marc Cosentino's book, Case in Point, explores market sizing questions in very great detail. So, you definitely want to pick up that book and leverage that. And also, brain teasers. Now, you know, brain teasers like why are manhole covers round?

How many golf balls can you fit in a 747? Or actually how much paint would it take to paint a 747, sort of brain teaser questions. I can tell you with regard to brain teasers, I only saw one brain teaser pop up in the last 4 years from one firm. So it's not likely that you'd get one, but there's a possibility you will, so you want to familiarize yourself with that, and in this training series, we will not go to practice brain teasers.

So from the perspective of prepping, business cases, Of course, any case that you get on the internet from a school case pack from one of the case prep books. Those are business cases, but you also need to familiarize yourself with practice market sizing and at least practice a couple of brain teasers.

Understand Business Cases

I've separated the business case into seven subtopics. These topics can cover the most frequently used business scenarios, ranging from increasing profitability to acquisition, from organizational behavior to market analysis.

You must remember, though, that these seven categories are not mutually exclusive or completely exhaustive. A market entry case may require industry analysis. An acquisition case may also involve evaluating return on investment. There are some cases which may not fit neatly into any of the major business case types as they have elements from one or more of them.

What Is A Decision Tree And How To Use It

Before we move into solving the main cases and teaching you how to build proper structures to solve them, I think it's valuable to spend some time talking about the mechanics, structure and logic behind some of the tools and techniques we would use. I want you to be quite comfortable with the fact that as we introduce you to decision trees and some of the underlying concepts, you'll not fully understand it at this point, but you'll probably understand it a lot better when you see it applied in the forthcoming chapters.

As we use them within complete cases, the reason I'm introducing it to you is so you get familiar with the techniques and concepts and the language and why we do things the way we do them. Now, let me just explain what decision trees are. Let's assume I asked you to explain to me how Toyota could increase its revenue. Now, if you've already been reading up on management consulting cases and doing some pre reading, you'd probably use a profitability framework. But if you hadn't become familiar with the way consulting cases are done, you'd probably start brainstorming some exercise.

You'd start throwing out ideas, You'd say things like Better cars, better prices, more models, more products, fix the supply chain, lower salaries, promotions. And maybe you'd come up with something like manufacturing in China. That's what most people do. When you ask them to solve a problem, they start brainstorming ideas because throughout kindergarten, primary school, high school, university, you're taught to brainstorm by throwing out ideas. I'm sure you've heard this refrain whereby a brainstorming exercise is one whereby you're not meant to criticize. You're going to throw out an idea, put together a large list, and then grow through it.

You're taught to be unstructured because apparently for many people, being unstructured is the equivalent of being innovative. So they believe if you are unstructured, you are very innovative and they encourage you to just throw out these ideas. And this is what you get at the end of the day. Now, how can Toyota increase profitability? You start throwing out these ideas, but let me explain to you what a decision tree is and why it's used. A decision tree is useful for a number of reasons. The first reason is it brings structure.

And you've heard this term a billion times before that you should be more structured because being structured shows causality, cause and effect. If you state something, you must be able to show what causes it and what effect it has on something else. It allows you to understand the scope of the problem. This is how far the problem extends and the depth of the problem, how deep it goes. Now let's take the Toyota profitability issue here. Profits are driven by revenue and costs. Revenue is driven by either product one product to product three or could be split down into price and volume. Volume is driven by promotional activity, product mix and the place of availability of the product. In a way, the availability in the supply chain and the price is doing a number of things as well.

The question you might ask me is why would we choose to split revenue by product here and by price? But let's assume you've got three different product mixes, auto trucks, financing. Clearly, if I had to put price in volume after revenue, I'd have to summarize, I'd give an average for the auto price, the truck price and the price on vehicle financing, which gives me nothing useful. It's better when you have multiple product lines to break down revenue first by product, then examine each product by price and volume. But we're getting ahead of ourselves. Let's just put down costs a little bit further.

Again, you can split it by product or fixed costs or variable costs. You can split fixed costs even further into labor, rent, depreciation and what have you. And I think about it this way, you can see very quickly here that profitability is directly driven by revenue and cost. In fact, revenue minus cost gives you profitability, product one plus product two plus product three gives you revenue price times volume gives you revenue. The impact of promotions and the mix plus placement gives you volume labor plus rent plus depreciation gives you fixed costs. Fixed costs plus variable costs gives you costs. What's this doing for you? Well, firstly, it's creating a very clear structure in your mind in terms of what drives the revenue. But why is that important?

For example, we spoke about promotion. You'd not go to the meeting and tell the client. We decided to explore promotion because it sounded interesting and people thought it was worth pursuing. Why would you choose to move to promotion if this is your main question you're solving? This is level one, then level two, then level three, level four. Why would you pick a level four issue to fix? You bypass volume, you bypass revenue, you bypass costs, you bypass fixed costs, you bypass variable costs. Why would you pick revenue down here at the fourth level as something worth your time to examine?

It's not worth your time because you don't know it's the issue. You have to first eliminate different options. So a decision tree provides structure, profit, revenue costs. It allows you to put a mathematical symbol between it. It shows causality. You can clearly see profits are driven by revenue costs, revenue is driven by the different product mixes or price times volume. It gives you the scope. Of the problem. On one page you can see all the different issues that are driving profitability and you can see the depth of the issue. You can see how fine the organization is. This way the issue extends all I want you to take away from this part is that a decision tree allows you to break down problems logically.

Now, let me show you this. Let's assume we brainstorm fixed revenue and cut labor costs. You can see that labor and revenue are not on the same level. When you're talking about issues, talk about them at the same level. And when you move to a different level, you should make sure the interviewer knows you have moved to the next level. So how do you do this? Let's brainstorm using this approach. How can we increase profitability?

We can either increase profitability by cutting down costs and increasing revenue, but we don't know anything about cost structure revenue. We can start from either side. So we'll start from the revenue side, which can either increase the revenue with its fastest growing product category or increase revenue with the smallest growing product category, or if Toyota only has one product category, we can look at increasing the price of the product category or increasing the volume. Now we've looked at revenue. Let's look at costs, either reduce fixed costs or reduce variable costs. If we want to reduce fixed costs, we can look at labor, rent and depreciation. Now what we're going to do is we're going to show you the different kinds of decision trees you get so you have a better understanding of how to actually use them. There are four types of decision trees.

One, you're not going to use that much. And it's actually where the term decision tree came from. But from the other three, you'll use them extensively. And the key thing here is don't worry about understanding this perfectly, understand the logic and the thinking here. But as we go through the cases, you will see how decision trees are used in follow up chapters. We'll explain why we use decision trees and not hypotheses. What are the differences between decision trees and hypotheses and how can you use them together? Decision trees are a far more powerful technique and they're used by all the major management consulting firms. So let's look at the four types of decision trees you'll encounter. It's a question: Should you go shopping or not? If yes, do you go to a mall or do you go to a single store or not? Okay.

You go to a single store. Do you go to a clothing store or a shoe store? And that's the way you break it down. They're not very common in consulting cases. They're probably the least common kinds of decision tree You build in the brainstorming chapter. We'll use this sort of decision tree to help Toyota increase productivity. Let's look at another, let's look at how to fly to Spain. The options available to you are Delta and Emirates and Southwest Airlines. Now, this decision is different in the sense that you have your options laid out for you. There's no particular yes or no. It's very similar to this, but the options are laid out for you. You can either choose option one, option two, option three, but you'll never choose one and two, because you only want to fly there once.

You can either choose Delta or Emirates or Southwest. So this one here forces you to choose one option and the other kind of decision tree. How to increase profits? When you increase profits, you can either go for revenue or costs. But the interesting thing is you can choose two paths. You can choose to increase profit by increasing revenue and lowering costs. And then the final kind of decision tree that you'll work on is something that's a bit tougher to understand. So don't worry if you don't. Now it's a sequential decision tree in a sequential decision tree, we don't give you the details. Let's say you should just know Company A enters a new market.

The decision tree may have step one. Step two, step three, step four, step five. But to use this decision, you cannot stop at step four. You have to start at step one and work your way down. Now, this will only make little sense to you Now. It's very difficult to explain without an example. So we're not going to do it for the sake of your case. You should know that this kind of decision tree is available and we're going to use these kinds of decision trees in this training series. In chapters, we'll teach you how to use these kinds of decision trees.

Why To Create Hypotheses With Decision Tree

In this chapter series, we built our entire approach around decision trees. In fact, when I was a consulting partner or associate, I dealt with my cases using decision trees and they were very successfully done. And most firms you join, you have an option of either using the hypothesis led approach or the decision tree led approach. They're different, but you can use them to get into it. I'm going to show you how to use hypotheses. Then I'm going to show you how I thought these are difficult to use and how you can use a hypothesis with a decision tree.

Let's just start off hypothesis is something most people don't understand. So I'll tell you up front what I see. Most people will tell me something like profits are dropping. So firstly, let me draw a diagram and I'll explain to you how to structure hypotheses. What's the statement? Due to a snowstorm, trucks are delayed, which is an observable phenomenon. And the impact is the fact that because of the delay, they arrive late, which means clothing cannot get onto the shelves of Walmart on time.

Now, when you write out the hypothesis, you should always have three parts due to a snowstorm. The trucks are delayed, leading to clothing being put on the shelves late. Now, why do you need these three parts? Why Part A? Part B, Part C? Think about it. You need this so you can test the hypothesis. Now, once you have the hypothesis, the next step is to draw a set of graphs, usually 1 to 3. Think what you put on the x axis and the y axis to test it out. The question is on one axis here, you can say there's a correlation between lateness of trucks and snowstorms, the same test you can do for a delayed truck. So call it lateness or whatever term you want and clothing not on your shelves.

And that allows you to prove your hypothesis with one that can prove or disprove it when people tell you things. And my hypothesis is that the company's profits are down because it's not making the product correctly. You've only fulfilled two of the criteria, but you must fulfill three. What's the observable phenomenon? What's causing the observable phenomenon and what is the observable phenomenon causing? What's the impact? You must have three parts to it. So let me explain to you why that's so difficult to work with. In fact, when you join as a management consultant, you may join us at MBA level, associate at McKinsey, and you'll know that hypotheses are very hard to be messy and difficult to work with. Consultants take a long time to learn how to use them.

What I thought this was was due to the snowstorm. Trucks are arriving late, causing delays in clothing. Now let's assume we had another hypothesis. Say something along the lines of due to unsynchronized brakes. The unpack is a packet of clothing in the store that is not available when trucks arrive. They're causing delays in the clothing display. Now, the other hypothesis is that due to late displays, items can't remain on full price long enough, which leads to a drop in revenue. Now these are all well crafted hypotheses. I mean, if you came up with them, you were doing a great job. But let me ask you a question.

How do you know that when you're testing this hypothesis, you're testing it independently of the other two? So first, let's get back to being messy.

Let's look at the collectively exhaustive side. How do you know you've captured all the issues collectively? Exhaustive means, all the issues or the full scope of issues. How do you know you have the full scope of issues and how do you know they're independent? And if I change something here, how do I know I'm not changing something else in other drivers? Secondly, I can't see if they're mutually exclusive because it's very difficult to see what makes up the mechanics of each hypothesis and whether a part of that calculation is replicated in another hypothesis. So understanding the difficulty we've had here, let's look at the same problem, but use a decision tree and then show how to build the processes into a decision tree. So I'm going to show you how to solve this problem. Again, using a decision tree.

We haven't even gotten into the case training yet. We're just talking about the basic underpinnings here of how to solve cases. As we move into proper case training, you'll see how to apply these concepts. What I do here is assume the company wants us to fix profits, so we'll break down profits into revenue and costs. Now, there are reasons why I'd pick revenue or cost to start off with and you have to have a good reason for doing it. I'm not going to explain this for now. I just want to show you why decision trees are more effective than hypotheses and how you can use them together while still being led by a decision tree. So let's assume we start on the revenue side.

Let's use a different one, which was created by Kenichi Ohmae, a former McKinsey senior partner. I like the framework very well, very common, but it's one of the most powerful. So let's say take market share, expand into new markets. Now you notice there's more than one framework. I could have used the four P's here, but what drives volume? Let's think about this. What drives volume? Think about it logically. You either have more stores or more volume through stores. More stores. Let's assume it's not on the cards to have more. The company doesn't have the money. How do you push more volume through more stores? You either have more items or the same number. Of items selling faster.

We know that speed is not the issue. The company is going to tell us that speed isn't the issue. How do you have more items? You can either have more items delivered or you can have them packed into the store. Actually, for more items, I'd say you could have them packed into the store. I'd say here a more logical step would be to say a greater variety. And how do you get more items into the store? Well, either through shipping more, keeping less in the warehouse. How do you ship more? You either have more trucks or bigger trucks. You can very clearly see the scope of the problem. You can see I've eliminated the key drivers. It's clear to you why you've eliminated them.

And it's also very easy to see that if you wanted to send more trucks, there's one of two options. You want to increase the number of trucks that don't have any impact on the variety of products. It allows you to test the Me side and the sea side much better because you can very quickly do everything that logically includes volume and the same thing for profit and the same thing for costs. And if you're introduced to a hypothesis here, you know it's mutually exclusive because it specifically covers this point. And more likely, the hypothesis is very focused. It's not like you come up with 6 or 7 and you don't know which is right. You've already eliminated the unnecessary options. This is a very focused hypothesis.

All you have to do now is test it with your graph. So build the graph and test it. That's all you do. So it's a very simple process. Search data for the X and Y axis. You're going to give the client your recommendation. So remember, using decision trees to generate hypotheses is far more accurate than first creating a hypothesis directly and I've proven it to you. If you want to use hypotheses, you're welcome to. You can solve cases with both approaches, Of course, but I find decision trees to be far more structured, far more disciplined, and far more guiding for you.

McKinsey vs. BCG Case

In today's episode, we're going to cover the McKinsey versus Bain approaches. And I'm really excited about doing this because what I've noticed is that many of our clients are struggling to understand how to change between the McKinsey approach or the Bain approach first and the BCG facilitated brainstorming approach. And rather than simply talking people through this difference, I thought it would be a good idea to do a chapter on this so people could explicitly follow and understand what's happening here, because it's an important technique.

It's a technique you could use in a BCG case if you wanted, but certainly you're never going to bypass Bain and McKinsey interviews unless you can apply this very, very well. So let's talk about what the differences are between McKinsey and Bain as a group. And then BCG is the other. We'll talk about the differences. And then based on these differences, we'll explain how to use the McKinsey Bain answer first approach, which is very similar. It's actually built off the BCG approach. So let's start with the first one who's leading the case in a McKinsey case or a BCG case? The McKinsey case is led by an interview.

You'll have to present your thinking and the interviewer will tell you how to proceed. In the case of BCG, you'll guide the interviewer through your thinking. So beyond that, there's also the style of the cases for BCG known as facilitated brainstorming and McKinsey. It's an answer first approach. So what is facilitated brainstorming? You're basically going to be working with the interviewer as opposed to the interviewer simply assessing you. That's a very big difference with BCG. Rather than an interview and knowing the answer up front and you just giving them what they need, you'll work with the interviewer to sketch out the problem and build it. With McKinsey. They have answers and you need to present your solution that matches what they're looking for.

And the analogy here is I always think of old English mazes like garden mazes, where you have a sculpture cut up to look like a maze, and then you walk through the shrubbery. In a BCG case, the partner or the interviewer is with you in the maze, but you're holding their hand and you're leading them and they're helping you think things through. And that's why it's called facilitated brainstorming. They facilitate your brainstorming. But in a McKinsey case, imagine the McKinsey interview is nowhere in the maze with you. They're sitting somewhere else and you've got a microphone in your ears and they're asking you what you're doing and why you're doing it. So I find that with a BCG person, it's a lot easier to solve a case because you solve it with them. But with a McKinsey person, you solve it for them.

Now, the other one is clarity. In the McKinsey case, it's very specific. What the key question is, they don't hide that. They don't make it difficult to understand. They tell you very clearly this is the problem. This is what we want you to fix. There's no other issue here. But the BCG case is not always clear. Sometimes it is, but sometimes it's not. In most BCG cases, they're testing your conceptual ability to sketch out the problem and then solve it. In a McKinsey case, they're telling you the problem. They want you to fix it. There's a very big difference here. And fourth is the amount of data provided for BCG. It's very small for McKinsey and Bain. There is a ton of data provided to you. In fact, there's so much that you need to ask clarifying questions up front now.

Five I think there's some other differences between these interviews beyond the issues I've mentioned up front among the amount of data presented and so on. I think the other thing you notice with the McKinsey style is they're very structured in what they're looking for. You have to present what they're looking for as opposed to coming up with an innovative solution that they may be open to. But BCG is kind of developing it with you. And because the answer isn't clear, if you come up with a good answer, it's not on the list of prescribed solutions. They'd still be okay with it. So knowing the things you know, how would you go about the case? In a typical case, in step one, you'd normally take some time to gather your thoughts and ask clarifying questions. So step one is taking time.

You do the same thing in the McKinsey case. You take time to come up with clarifying questions. Two You'll ask fewer clarifying questions, much fewer. Because unlike a BCG case where much less data is given to you in a McKinsey case, so much has been presented to you that the odds of you having to ask substantial qualifying questions is minimal. Three Once you've asked your clarifying questions, you need to come up with the key question generally then a McKinsey case because the key question is obvious. You don't have to rephrase anything they've already given you. If the key question is explicit in the McKinsey case, because so much data is already given to you, you don't have to ask a question to develop your structure.

You're expected to do it with very little information. And this is where a BCG case and a McKinsey case differ. The BCG case. You'll develop your high level structure, you'll ask clarifying questions and then build it out again until you identify what the problem is. From that problem, you'll develop option one. Option two, option three. And that's where the McKinsey and BCG approach diverge. The first big difference is in the McKinsey case, because so much information is provided to you, they expect you to develop your structure without providing anything else. It's known as the bartering technique.

If someone offers you something, you have to offer them back. McKinsey has offered you so much, you can't come back and then offer them more questions. You have to offer a structure. So in a McKinsey case, you build out your structure using the information, provided you prioritize certain branches. And for those of you who don't know how to prioritize, you prioritize drivers on sensitivity to the original question. You're solving the original question. You have to ask yourself, How important is that branch? And driving that answer, prioritize the most important ones and for each of them develop a hypothesis. And then for each hypothesis, get the graph you want to draw to test it based on the graph you want to draw, you can then ask for data until the interview. This is my hypothesis.

This is the kind of analysis I would want to do. This is the data that will need to run the hypothesis. And then the McKinsey interviewer will either confirm your hypothesis and say, Well, this is the data, tell me what you do now. And then you'd work from that point on so you can see the differences Now. Why do you want to build your hypothesis on the decision tree? Well, let's think about it. The biggest problem with building hypotheses is that they are extraordinarily messy. I mean, they're horrible to work with. When MBA candidates want to give me hypotheses, they just throw out ridiculous statements and some overlap. So they build someone like this, one like that. They build another hypothesis and it just overlaps.

If you build your hypothesis wound around one part of the decision tree, you're guaranteed to make sure it's messy because your decision tree will be messy and it's not going to overlap. So we'll take that theory and show you how to develop it. We're going to take this case. I'm going to apply all of this theory to show you how to do it and understand that, you know, very verbal explanations when we give them to candidates, they're not that easy to follow. So we think these chapters, the next few McKinsey chapters that will follow, will be a good way for people to understand how to do McKinsey cases.

How To Succeed In Case Interviews

How to succeed in case interviews You are expected to develop a creative, customized approach to solve the problem. I'm going to talk a little bit more about how you can create this creative approach, but something to keep in your mind right now, whether you've started practicing or going to be starting practice soon. You need to come up with your own customized approach to solve the problem.

Now, you are going to leverage, perhaps Porter's five forces, you may leverage the three C's, you may leverage Marc Cosentino's Case in Point, it's called the IVK system, you are going to leverage that, but you're not going to use that exclusively. So this is an important point, you cannot walk into an interview and say, 'Well, I'm going to leverage, I'm going to use Porter's five forces to solve this problem.' You cannot do that. You also have to show that you're intellectually curious and you genuinely enjoy the process. And I think this is a good way for you to self-select out of recruiting preparation. If you start to practice cases and you really don't like it, you are probably not going to be successful in the case interview, and perhaps you may not even like the actual work in the consulting industry. So, you get to genuinely enjoy the case process and be very intellectually curious and enjoy the problem-solving process.

More importantly, You have to demonstrate strong business acumen, regardless of the topic. You don't have a business background, but that doesn't mean that you haven't done research and homework on business topics and current business issues. So, one of the things you need to start doing is read the newspaper. You know, New York Times, Wall Street Journal and Bloomberg for most of the regions, for European candidates, you can also read Financial times and Reuters. The report on business, read the business chapter so that you understand the business issues and topics that are salient in the market right now. You have to show poise and confidence throughout the case even when pressed. You know, Of course, they are going to put a little bit of pressure on you. How do you manage that?

You need to be able to manage through that very comfortably. Passion for problem-solving, I think that speaks a little bit to the intellectual curiosity and genuinely enjoying the process, but you have to be really energetic and excited about the problem that they're giving you, and that solves that. One thing I wanted to add to the passion for problem-solving, I mean, an example of how you can demonstrate this. I know that at the end of every case, I was genuinely interested to know and I asked the consultant, they said, 'you have any questions for me?' and I would say, 'yeah, I have a quick, sort of preliminary question, the case you gave me, was this a case you worked on, and what was the outcome?' And I was genuinely curious to know. So that you know that sort of an example of being passionate and curious, and enjoying the consulting process.

Next Steps

In this chapter Book, we've seen how to solve different types of case studies. Case interviews for McKinsey, Bain and BCG can be really hard and most of the interviewers are intimidating. Fortunately, solving business cases, estimation and brainstorming is straightforward and completely doable, as we've seen in the Book. By following the steps outlined in each chapter, you can easily sort out the ways to define scope, create a structure or issue tree and build hypotheses to make those final recommendations.

This brings us to the end of our chapter Book on management consulting Case Essential Training. As you continue your journey. There are many great resources available. Some of my favorites are the McKinsey problem solving test, a multiple choice test that will demonstrate your analytical skills and is used as a complement to our problem solving interviews. The other resource I'd highly recommend is BCG Consultant interview preparation and practice cases. It's an interactive place to find out a sample BCG case interview, question and process.

The final website you can go for a visit is consulting interviews at Bain, where you can find a lot of interview preparation materials and chapters to help you nail your consulting interview. I really hope you've enjoyed this Book. If you've got any questions or comments or if you're just looking to practice your problem solving skills, I'd love to hear from you.

How To Become A Great Management Consultant

A Final Note: How to Become a Great Management Consultant Key success factors Baseline analytical expertise, but also... Excellent interpersonal skills and knowledge of people management facilitation motivating others conflict management Frank self-awareness of strengths and weaknesses Receptiveness to feedback from a variety of sources Ability and willingness to act on feedback training experimentation practice Desire to succeed as a consultant The function of expectations in predicting consultant success.

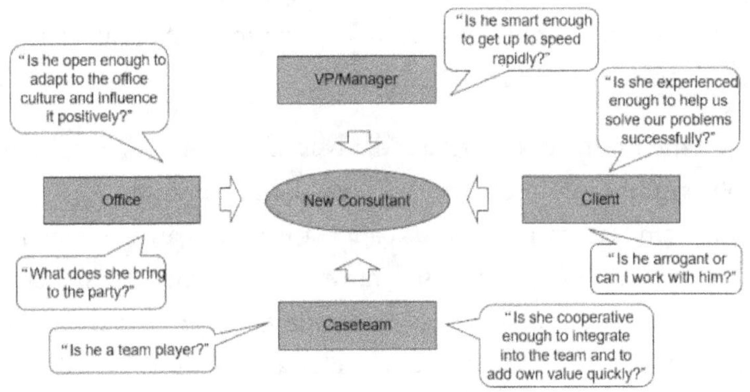

A successful consultant... "Few consultants have the total package when they arrive. The best consultants leverage either extraordinary analytical or client skills and then develop the rest over time." "Paradoxically, team skills are not a way that consultants distinguish themselves. Almost everyone we hire has excellent team skills based on where and how we recruit."

"Over time, there is no substitute for the ability to quickly crack a tough business problem/analysis and design/execute an efficient path for gathering the data to back it up.

This is what we do day in and day out. It creates client success stories and smooth team operations." Unsuccessful consultants... ...are arrogant and unreceptive to feedback. They stop three-quarters of the way through the analysis because they are confident it's right and don't convince skeptical clients to change." ...do not become experts in the functional or industry area they are working in. The clients question their value-added - often from their first interaction." ...do not get out in front of their managers. They are executing another person's 'to do's' rather than designing their own path. They don't live up to, let alone exceed, expectations. Their lifestyle is totally reactive.

And their morale is understandably low." ...treat the consulting job as an extension of school. Like Books and professors, cases and team leaders are good or bad. Case work is an assignment, not a personal mission. Also, they think in terms of 'us/them' rather than joining the team and pulling for the joint cause. As a result, they do not add as much value as they think they do, or they're capable of, and they are tiresome to manage." Managing expectations for new consultants.

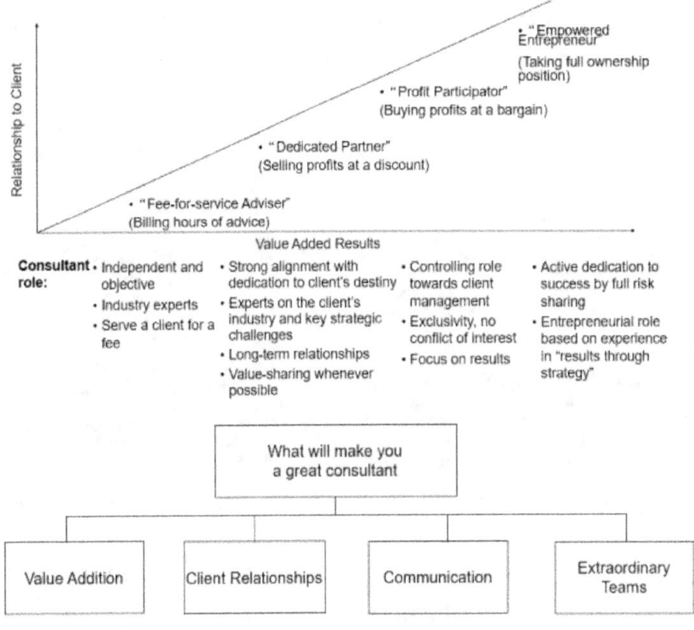

Consultant role:	• Independent and objective • Industry experts • Serve a client for a fee	• Strong alignment with dedication to client's destiny • Experts on the client's industry and key strategic challenges • Long-term relationships • Value-sharing whenever possible	• Controlling role towards client management • Exclusivity, no conflict of interest • Focus on results	• Active dedication to success by full risk sharing • Entrepreneurial role based on experience in "results through strategy"

What will make you a great consultant

Value Addition	Client Relationships	Communication	Extraordinary Teams

What do we expect from you as a new consultant in the area of value addition?

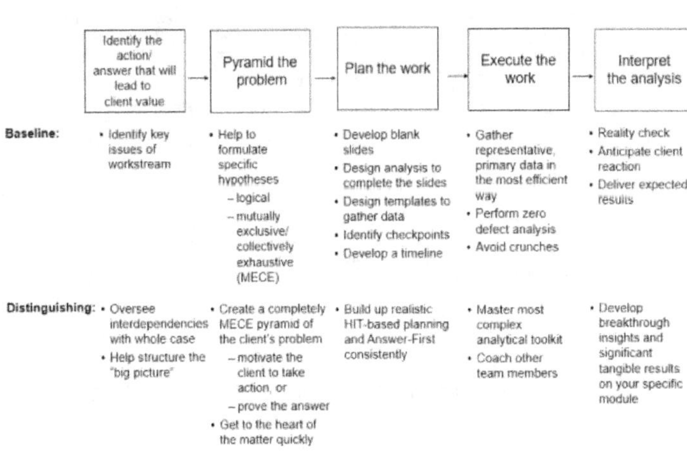

	Identify the action/answer that will lead to client value	Pyramid the problem	Plan the work	Execute the work	Interpret the analysis
Baseline:	• Identify key issues of workstream	• Help to formulate specific hypotheses – logical – mutually exclusive/ collectively exhaustive (MECE)	• Develop blank slides • Design analysis to complete the slides • Design templates to gather data • Identify checkpoints • Develop a timeline	• Gather representative, primary data in the most efficient way • Perform zero defect analysis • Avoid crunches	• Reality check • Anticipate client reaction • Deliver expected results
Distinguishing:	• Oversee interdependencies with whole case • Help structure the "big picture"	• Create a completely MECE pyramid of the client's problem – motivate the client to take action, or – prove the answer • Get to the heart of the matter quickly	• Build up realistic HIT-based planning and Answer-First consistently	• Master most complex analytical toolkit • Coach other team members	• Develop breakthrough insights and significant tangible results on your specific module

What do we expect from you as a new consultant in the area of client relationships?

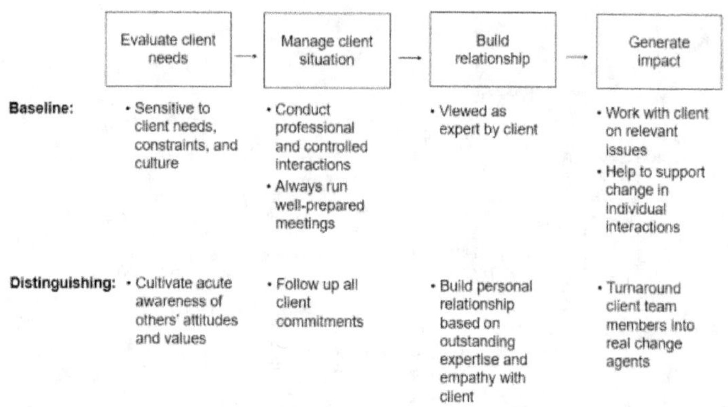

What do we expect from you as a new consultant in the area of communication?

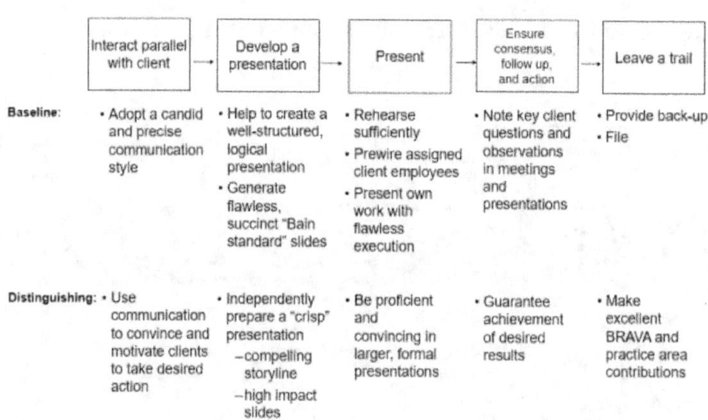

Evolving expectations for experienced consultants

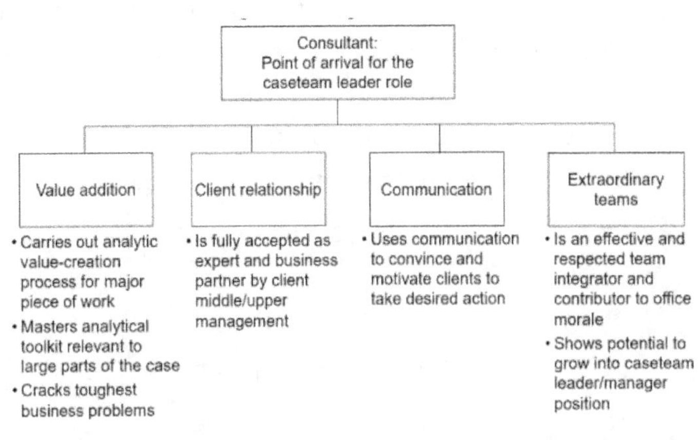

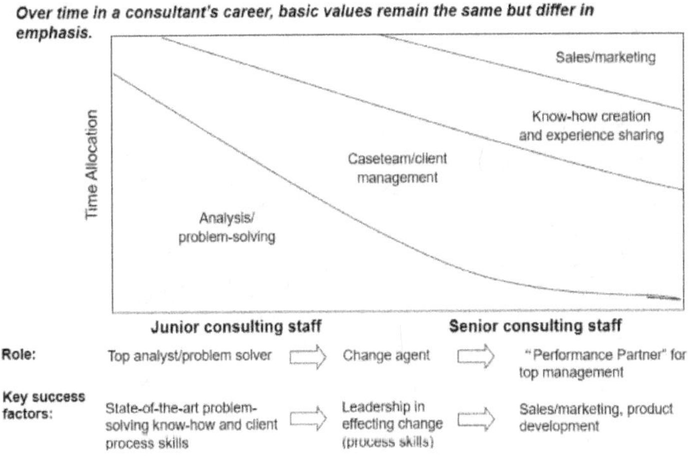

Key takeaways execute on more than good analysis develop excellent interpersonal and people management skills self-assess for areas of potential growth use feedback to achieve full potential proactively manage case team work, managers, and clients are aware of career milestones and their shifting roles, and actively manage transitions capitalize on opportunities to go beyond baseline performance to achieve distinguishing results in value addition, client relationships, communication, and extraordinary teams integrate case team work and firm asset-building into personal and professional aspirations.

Logistics and Ocean Shipping in Supply Chain Management

This Book is for the ones who are working in Logistics, Supply Chain, Export and Import part of Supply Chain industry this Book will help you gain knowledge about Ocean Logistics Management and multimodal transport operations in depth covering interesting topics like Container stuffing, Types of Ships for Container Logistics and Shipping, Types of Containers etc the instructor of this Book has kept this Book very practical no textbook definitions and boring theory.

As container shipping is the heart of Global trade and Logistics and Supply Chain, Learning about Ocean Logistics will help you gain insights of the container shipping and ocean Logistics industry. As 90% of the world's cargo is moved by Ocean Logistics and 60% by container which speaks volume of the role of Liner shipping in Logistics and Supply Chain.

We have tried to keep the Book as simple as possible to keep the complex definitions of Logistics and Supply Chain Management simple Logistic and Supply Chain professional around the globe hold respected position in many companies such as Logistics and Supply Chain service provider, Logistics and Supply Chain department in International Export and Import companies due to evolution of modern day trade the Logistics and Supply Chain industry requires more and more skilled Logistics and Supply Chain professionals

The device which you are using may be imported by containers that is why Ocean shipping is the base of logistics and Supply Chain for your Inventory Management. So let's get started with the wonderful industry of Ocean shipping in Logistics and Supply Chain and become an asset to the National and Global Economies.

Introduction

Hi there, thanks for joining me again. This Book is about how to deliver on time, the material or service, how to do a proper expediting. This seems very easy, but within 15 years of my experience, I have noticed many people do not have the right skills. They do not have the right approach to the issue. And at the end of the day, this falls into your shoulders and there will be additional cost, late delivery. So operationally, it could be a disaster.

Financially, it could be a disaster. And now I'm going to give you all the tools you will need for you to avoid the situation and to come up with a strong expediting and delivering outstanding service to the company. Please join me right now. I will explain how.

What will you learn from this Book?

A) Expediting & Shipping Strategy You will discover that there are multiple strategies associated with concepts that will guide you for your entire professional experience. You will be guided on when and how to apply the techniques that will make you be extremely efficient with good quality work and smooth expediting. That will cover the moment the order is issued till the material is delivered/ service rendered and supplier paid.

B) Tactical Expediting & Shipping Management Tools throughout the process I will share with you tools & concepts that I have personally used successively within several companies during 15 years that are easy to use and guarantee a minimum effort for 0 delay in your Supply Chain. That will cover the moment the order is issued till the material is delivered/ service rendered and supplier paid.

C) Develop your skills and gain recognition internally you will be able to manage the expediting of multiple items/services for different projects in parallel and hence increase your management and expediting skills abilities. Make a difference fast!

The Various Types of Expediting and when do you use each.

There are different ways of doing a proper expediting, so I will show to you the different modes of expediting and you will have to apply the proper expediting on each case as applicable.

The Desk Expediting

The first expediting mode, the most famous of all, is the desk expediting. So what is it? It's simply the activity of expecting from your own office, either through email or by phone. And this is obviously not a costly solution at all. OK, it does not involve any kind of travel. So it has advantages.

However, it is usually utilized for low critical materials or low value items because it could be a bit more risky or less efficient than also kind of expediting. I will give you a few tools in case you have a limited budget and you cannot have a different kind of expedition.

I have for you some tools which will allow you to do a proper desk expediting. So keep focus. Stay with me.

The Field Expediting

The second way of doing and expediting is what we call field expediting. So what is it? It is usually the case where you do a field expediting whenever you have a long lead time, or item which is critical, and for which there are multiple milestones involving procurement, engineering, fabrication.

In all those cases, you would be required to go to the supplier office fabrication shop and follow up all the key milestones to avoid any slippage. And if there are any, obviously you have to address immediately and ask for a mitigation action plan to recover from any delay in advance.

Obviously, this is the whole idea of expediting. The delay should not come to you as a surprise. You have to be there for this key milestone. This is what I think is expediting.

The Resident Expediting

The first case is what we call resident expediting. So what is the resident expediting? In this scenario, You will have an expeditor full time at the supplier office, not only for key milestones but somebody full time.

It's obviously an added pressure for the supplier and you'll have to agree to that. But this means that it's a very, very critical item for you, that you cannot afford any single day of delay and you have the resources to be a full time supplier.

So this is an expensive, you know, expediting, but it is very effective because you are fully aware, fully in control. You should not have as much as deviation to the planned activity.

Third Party Expediting

The last type of expediting is what we call third party expediting. So what is a third party expediting? it's actually either a field expediting for a specific milestone, either a resident expediting for a full time period. But it is not done by you nor your company.

It is done by a professional expediting service of a company very well known in the market. There are so many of them. I can give you a few names, but you can Google it. You will find very well known companies. And this company will do for you a complete expediting with reports and the format that you are looking for. And he will follow up all the steps on your behalf.

And for example, it's very much used if you have expedited it overseas. The supplier is done, is based overseas and you do not want to travel or you do not have the resources or you do not have the time, or maybe there is a visa issue. You directly contact this company and usually those companies are established globally. So they will have an office in the country and they will send an expediter for you to do the job.

Low Risks / Low Value Items

Hi there! we are talking about low risk material and low value material .In this case, you will obviously do on your desk aspirating as you have seen, and you will only simply, you know, once you have issued the PO, that the acknowledgement has been done, the data have been agreed upon, only follow up either on email or on the phone a few days before delivery, because in any case, this is low risk, means most of the cases You have a delivery in a couple of days and you are not expecting any kind of delay.

High Risk/ High Value Items

So in this scenario, you have a high risk on the expediting activities. IT could be a long lead material. It could be a high value item. So in those cases, you have to be very careful and you have to deal with a professional expediting because your company is at risk. You can impact your operations. OK, so how are you going to do it?

First of all, you need to monitor, manage and control frequently as much as required. OK, it could be as a minimum monthly, could be weekly or daily in some cases. OK, and this you ll have in addition to calls obviously, you ll have reports, which I'm sharing to you, that you will insure the supplier will be filling it with the required backup documentation.

For example, in this report, you ask to ensure that he has completed his sub procurement activities. So you will ensure that you ll receive the unpriced, signed order from his sub vendor for the key purchasing, for the key sub equipment, for example, it's not for everything. Of course, you cannot ask so many sub orders, no. But maybe there are two, three, five key sub orders that will ensure that you will be on time for his own procurement activities. You ask for the unpriced copies, this is a must.

The whole activity of the monitoring should be done comparing the planned activities , the planned dates with the actual dates. And if there is no mismatch, then that's OK. If there is a mismatch, the supplier needs to highlight it to you and you need to immediately ask for a plan. Right. I mean, a recovery plan with maybe additional resources for him to finish on time. Could be additional manpower, additional equipment. Sometimes they ask for a rush fee, whatever it is, you need to push the supplier.

And as soon as you get the report, to get his plan in place for him to recover on the next report, OK. So at the end of the day, he can still deliver on time. Or if there is a delay, it is a minimum delay, not a huge delay. This is the whole point of expediting. This is what you have to do in case of critical procurement. Please have a look at all the forms and share it with you. It is absolutely useful. I have done it for 15 years in all the companies I have been working for and there is nothing better than this.

The Complete Flow Chart of Expediting

Either we are going to see now the flowchart of expediting, because some of you may not be familiar with the notion of expediting, expediting the activity, which starts from the time the purchase order is issued to the time the material or service is actually received and paid for. OK, and I have seen many times that some Supply-Chain professionals just completely forget about it.

They just issue an order and then that is the thing. It's done. The job is done. This is only half done. OK, you need to go through the whole process. This is what you're going to see in this Book. And you can see on the attached flow chart each step. And we're going to go in detail in the key steps through separate chapters. You will go through it.

But, you know, basically you'll have to get the order, acknowledge you'll have to follow up for the production. You have to then arrange the collection and the shipping. Then you will have to follow up for the payment and the verification that the service is done. The material received at the end will have to close the order. OK, this is a whole flowchart of expediting.

Basic: Choose The Right Supplier

The number one reason is obviously, the selection of the supplier, so all starts with a proper prequalification and then within a bidding process, the selection of the right supplier. If you do select the right supplier, you will obviously have less issues or no issues at all in terms of delivery and your interaction will be minimal.

You will not need to be always behind the supplier. You will not need to take necessarily some preventive measures to ensure a delivery on time. So please pay attention to the prequalification and the selection of the supplier and I have a separate Book on that . You know, that is called how to ensure a purchasing and proper contracting strategy.

The Order / Contract Acknowledgement

A very well-known issue in contracting and procurement is the acknowledgement of the order or the contract. If you do not do your job properly, you have a major risk of delay or disputes due to that phase number one, which is the acknowledgement. So many times people do not pay attention to that step and just do the contract or the PO and stop it there.

Please do not ! Make sure you get a signed purchase order, signed and stamped. OK, on all pages. So that in case of dispute, you can always show the document that the supplier did acknowledge the or the contract. You cannot back down now. It is an official document between you two. And this is absolutely important. In case he does not acknowledge fully or he has some notes, you need to review and send it back to the supplier, confirming your acceptance.

If you do not agree, you need to issue a new document , discuss with the supplier, issue a new order or contract and get it stamped. Very important note is that the last document exchange between you two is the one valid legally. OK, it's not the first, it is always the last, so be the last to have that document received.

Have a Kick Off Meeting - KOM

Hi there. Let's talk about what we call a kickoff meeting. OK, you need to know what is a kickoff meeting and what is the whole purpose of a kickoff meeting, once you do a proper expediting and after the acknowledgement, this is the next step, Right. So the kickoff meeting, it's a meeting between all the stakeholders who are going to be concerned (involved) or handling this order. OK, so we are talking about the supplier.

Of course, the supplier has to be there, yourself, Of course. And possibly if you have in your company a document controller (if your package involves a lot of documentation during the fabrication stage), then you need the documentation controller there. You need the End-user related to that service we're going to receive from the supplier (the service or the material) so that the coordination can start and can be smooth during the whole process.

OK, so this is the main aim, to have a smooth execution and coordination of the order. And this is not necessarily required for no small value order, but for critical order, you have to go for this. Don't forget about this, because if you do, later on, you will see you will have a lot of issues of coordination and this will affect the schedule, Right. So you lose all benefit of Staying on track as per contractual due date, remember that.

Another point is that, the kick off meeting sometimes, could also in case of criticality and urgency, if you didn't receive the acknowledgement before, this is a time that you ll receive it from the supplier. The same day he signs it in front of you. OK, so this is closed. You verify that he acknowledged everything if the acknowledgement was not received prior, Right. So this is also another purpose of the kickoff meeting to make sure everything is in order, it is already signed so that we can move ahead with the production. And the last point is to plan the next step, Right. So you have your order with all milestones, all the deliveries, and also this time, you also explain to the supplier what you expect from them, Right. In terms of expediting.

For example, you will see later on, we have several reports that you will have to fill . So you agree with him or you tell him I need this report. Is it on a daily basis, Weekly basis, or monthly basis? But it is the time you explain to him what you expect, in which format to be sent, to whom, who has to be in copy and to whom he has to communicate, because the channel of communication is very important here. So this is a time you clarify all these things right, so Now you know exactly why you need a Kick-Off meeting and when necessarily, you don't need one.

Why You Need A Expediting Report

In the case of high value items which are having a long delivery time, you absolutely need an expediting report that will be filled out by your supplier on a regular basis. This engages the supplier and forces him to stick to the agreed contractual timelines. If you do not implement it and if there is no field expediting done, then you will be at a major risk of not having the accurate information on time, and risking delays on delivery.

Indeed the supplier if not engaged with a signed report could fool you and would discover at the last minute (too late) that the materials are not ready or have not been delivered on time. Since your company cannot afford such delays that would definitely impact operations substantially and make you look very bad in front of management, you need constantly those reports that will help you monitor the progress and be PROACTIVE Being an official document signed & stamped by supplier, in case of dispute and in front of a court this would represent the report would back up your claims that you may have with a supplier who would breach contractual or official commitments.

REPORT CONCEPT The report shall primarily compare the Planed Status resulting from the dates contractually agreed with the Actual status. Also it shall compare the two information / dates during each phases (From Engineering, Procurement, Fabrication, Inspection, Delivery) Note: Reports are to be associated with back up documents as proof of progress For example if supplier mentioned that 100% of raw material or Key suborders have been placed, he shall attach the unpriced suborders.

If he mentions that inspections/tests have been completed he shall attach a copy of those, or pictures of material ready. "unpriced" because it is confidential and the supplier shall not refuse to show you the order with an excuse that it is confidential. We only need to know that the suborder have been issued and ACKNOWLEDGED by the supplier

The Types Of Expediting Reports

What does the report shall contain? The Supplier's Progress Report shall contain: Forecast and actual progress (in %) of the engineering, procurement and manufacturing activities. Description of the activities performed during the month / weeks and the forthcoming month foreseen activities.

The manufacturing schedule which is a bar chart indicating the actual progress in the main events of the execution of the order in engineering, procurement and manufacturing (with major inspection steps if applicable). Procurement status that lists all the main components to be purchased or to be drawn from the stock with their required and actual delivery date, the selected Supplier.

Unpriced copy of main Suborders. Supplier invoice status which includes all invoices issued on the ORDER as of report date and status of release of payment against each invoice. The report shall be updated and sent periodically The Weekly Report Sample The Monthly Report Note: You can also if applicable have daily reports 19. What to do in case of a delay reported?

Let's say you have analyzed the situation, implemented the right expediting strategy, obtained a report from the supplier, however this time , the report shows many areas of concerns , and a mismatch between the planned dates and the actual dates. This is the time you need to step in , analyze the situation and immediately take the right action. You are racing against the clock, hence you shall not make a mistake and choose the right way to handle the situation.

Generally, there could be two situation only: 1) Situation of a Minor delay reported either by phone, expediting report / email 2) Situation of a Major delay reported either by phone, expediting report / email In the next two chapters, I will show you how you shall handle this in a professional manner , so that your company/performance do not get impacted.

Case of a Minor Delay Reported

In this situation, you got informed by the supplier on the report, maybe on a phone call, maybe on an email that they'll have maybe a minor delay. So you need, again, to decide quickly which action you're going to take. Number one, you need to assess with your end user the criticality, is this something critical or not? If it is not critical, if you can afford a few days of delay, nothing will change, then you may tell a supplier, OK, this is acceptable to proceed and agree on the revised delivery date. No problem.

Now, if that small delay will still be an issue for you. Then you need to take action quickly with a supplier, OK, so what are you going to do? You are going to review this report and understand the reasons for the delay. And check with him or maybe from his side if he proposes mitigation measures, OK, because you cannot afford two, three days of delay. It is too much and it's going to impact your operations. So you need to ask him for mitigation measures, action plan, right.

Whether he will put in additional resources, maybe additional manpower, material, or night shifts to finish on the short time that is left and ensure that the delay will be absorbed. And he will go back to the original delivery date, Right. This is the goal you need today or maybe it will come back to you with some additional cost or rush fee and so on. Again, you go back to the end user. If you say this is critical, I need it in any case.

Well, you need to pay for that. It is maybe minor, that extra amount of money that the supplier is asking you to deliver on time is maybe minor compared to the loss that this late delivery will generate. OK, so this is what you need to do in those cases.

Case of a Major Delay Reported

In case of major disruption on the schedule, you are obviously very dissatisfied. The supplier agreed on a delivery date. Now he is coming back to you saying that you will not be able to meet that target. And again, it will be delayed by maybe two, three weeks, one month or so, OK.

So you need to be very fast and make the right decision because every action counts. Every day of delay counts very much. Number one, you need to push the supplier as much as possible: phone calls, warning letters, meeting with suppliers, going to the supplier facility/ production facility, sending a third party to the supplier facility to do a field expediting, Right. So you will be knowing exactly, And pushing at all the stages to avoid any delay, All right.

This will put a lot of pressure on the supplier and it will have a very good impact. Aside from that, you can ask him for, again here, an action plan: how to recover, OK. What can he put on the table? Is it manpower, resources? all this you need to discuss with him and agree upon. And the last action is, if all this is not enough or not possible by the supplier, then we need to take a drastic action here. You might have to terminate that order, right.

Ask for some compensation and you might have to find another supplier, an alternate solution immediately, who can do the job On behalf of that supplier, (initial supplier contracted) but any cost additional, you will back charge it to the initial supplier. He was not able to do it, so you are arranging somebody else to do it for him, all right. But this has a cost , he will have to pay.

Make Sure To Have A Final Inspection Done

Hi there, so you have finished now, you know, the manufacturing process has been completed by the supplier, and you have maybe received some documentation, but then this is a time you have to execute the inspection if it is already agreed prior, on the order, right. So for the inspection you need to consider when you need an inspection, right, and how you're going to do it.

All right, we have here several kinds of expediting so we can refer to this Book further to the different kinds of expediting. So Inspection can be done during the manufacturing, but also at the end of the process, the most important one is at the end of the process. OK, so inspection has a cost, but has a major benefit. And the major benefit is that you do not import or you do not receive the material and you find out at the last minute that it is incomplete, it is broken, it is not exactly what you ordered and then you will lose all the time you'll have to ship it back ,repair and redo.

All this is time consuming. Quality has a cost. I mean, non quality has a cost. So to do quality work, we advise that you have an inspection done prior to collection. That inspection can be done by yourself, by a third party, whoever. He would go through the order, he would go through all deliverables and he would check the documentation and the material in front of him, right? So he will verify, for example, if it is a valve, that the certificate, is it adequate?

The material is in front of him, does it have the same fabrication? number Or whatsoever which can be linked to documentation. You verify that this is the job of the inspector. Once you finalize a job, you verify everything is in order to issue an IRC inspection release certificate. This is a first step for you to move ahead and do the next activity, which you will see soon. The coordination of the collection through a shipping release not.

The Shipping Release Note

Hi there, I would like to talk to you about a very efficient tool, which is called the Shipping Release Note, SRN. So what is an SRN ? SRN is a document where you list down the PO number or Contract reference, you list down the INCOTERM, OK, you then attach any associated document such as packing list or inspection release certificate (IRC) OK, and this is a document which will allow the supplier, allow the freight folder to move the cargo. OK, it's a shipping release note.

It allows for the release, why? Because you eliminate many risks here. Reason number one: You eliminate the risk of having the material stuck at the customs and pay all the demurrage charges. (associated) why, because you will verify beforehand, With the Freight forwarder that the documentation is accurate. And it will not get stuck. It is absolutely accurate and you have a proper delivery location, a proper consignee name, for example. OK, consignee name So you will issue the SRN only once this check has been done, not beforehand.

Number two, you are in control of the cost and mode of shipment because you decide, especially if it is a EX WORKS, if it is DAP Of course, if it is EX WORKS, for example, or FOB you can decide on the mode of shipment, right. You have the weight of the packing, you have the dimensions, if you want to go for sea freight because it's heavy and maybe more than 100 KG, you go for Sea Freight or road freight if you have the time. or if you want to go for airfreight because there's no time at all, then you have the budget to go airfreight. Then you go for air freight.

You decide and you put this information in the SRN itself so that SRN decides about or shows about the mode of shipment and all of the information related to the order. You eliminate the risk of having the material stuck. So you eliminate the time issue and you eliminate the cost issue by selecting the mode of shipment. This is why SRN is a key document and I have a sample for you. I'll be glad that you use it and I'm free to ask any questions you may have. Please use it.

It will save you a lot of time and money and it is very professional because it also keeps track of what is inside the box, because every document issued should have the SRN number on it. OK, your box has the SRN number, the packing list has the SRN number. So everybody knows at any point of time what is inside the box. Just referring to the document which is attached to the bucket list is very, very useful. Please use it.

How to Optimize Transportation Costs

So how are you going to do that? Number one, you should make sure that you have a contract in place for the freight forwarder to do all new shipping activities. And then once you have the cost known from your contracts, you can create your own tables so you can later on once you have the weight and dimensions just plug it into the table and find immediately, you know, the cost of sea freight for airfreight and then decide by yourself.

I have some stuff I'm sharing with you to help you do this activity by yourself. And now there is also the case where there is not necessarily a contract in place. You have to go to multiple freight forwarders. But to do that, we obviously need to know some information beforehand. So you should do your proper job as an expediter to collect on time, the weight and dimensions. OK, you know its location, you already know the INCOTERM from the other, but you do not know necessarily beforehand about the weight and the dimensions.

So I'm sharing with you one file that you need to get from the supplier with that information on that excel file all the time and ideally two weeks before the delivery time. So you have time to select the supplier for the freight and place an order and then do the coordination between the freight and the supplier. OK, this is key for successful expediting work, so please use my file for free and do this job properly.

Coordinate Closely With Your Appointed Freight Forwarder

Hi there, so now we have already issued the shipping release note to the supplier as well as a freight forwarder. So as an expediter, if there is no shipping department/logistics department, you have to liaise with the freight forwarder and the supplier to coordinate and have a smooth expediting and shipping process.

OK, so you follow up thanks to some kind of reports where you track where the material is. If it has been already, you know, collected in transit, is it at the Customs? For all this, you need to be fully aware as an expediter, and push in case of any delay anyway. This is your main role. Once the material arrives, then you verify that the inspection has been done on time. And again, there is no issue. If there is an issue, then you might have to return the material.

You have this overall short delivery report OSDR, so you monitor this with the supplier to replace the material. And commercially, you refer to the order, Of course, to have all the costs taken up by the supplier, not by you. This is your role. It has a cost If you don't do it well. It delays if you don't do it well. So please be on top of that and you will see if you are on top of that, you will be recognized internally and you will have a very professional quality work here.

Support Finance Whenever Required & Certify Invoices The Payment

After the delivery is done, or the service is completed, Well, the supplier will send the invoice. So it is your role to make sure that the whole process is smooth. In some companies the finance directly liaises with the supplier for invoice, that is fine. If it is not the case, you will have to push to get the invoice. So nothing gets delayed right now. If the invoice is not aligned with the order or the material delivered or the condition of the order, you will have yourself to push for a revised invoice. If it is not possible to issue a revised invoice and they have over invoiced, You ll need to ask for a credit note.

And your role is to verify that there is no mistake, but also the supplier is not abusing you. In a sense, you have done, let's say, the supplier has done a service, and in that service, it required six hours of work. But they have done only three hours and you have proof because it's signed, the Times sheet has been signed. It's very important for any service to have a signed timesheet for that purpose. So we have a proof, and the time sheet is showing only three hours.

But the supplier invoiced six, this is a case where you need to request for a credit note for the three hours balance which have been overcharged to you. This is your role to do all this process and it could be time consuming. So make sure you're always on top of this.

Have a PO Close Out Done

Hi There, this is a last phase in expediting :The PO CLOSE OUT. What is a PO close out? This is for critical PO, high value PO. But you need to check that everything has been completed from the supplier site, according to the order. The delivery has been done, service completed, he has delivered on time as per the order or not. If he has not delivered on time, then you need to calculate if you have in your order the close for penalty, for liquidated damages, for late delivery, you need to apply the amount as a penalty.

At least you need to calculate it. And then maybe your management can decide , do they want to apply? Yes or no. But you need to go through the history, when it was delivered, was it after the delivery date? you check again. What was the percentage LD applicable? How many days of delay? What was the value of the item late or service late? And you multiply, you calculate and you have a figure. At the end your manager needs to decide, does he want to charge a supplier or not? Maybe for commercial reasons he doesn't want to back charge or it's minor (value). OK, fine. But you need to do this work before you close out. Will you also verify if there was, for example, a bond to be submitted ,before, during ,at the end of the process?

Has the supplier submitted that bond? If not, this is a time to request the supplier to submit. If you did everything in order, then you can close the PO, right? So some companies have an internal form of allowing you. Some do not have, And it's only in SAP. In SAP, or Oracle or any ERP You tick, that means delivery is completed. That means everything is fine and we are not expecting any invoice.(further) Right. This is an internal process, but. You still have to get an official agreement from the supplier. This is key, right? People close out letters signed by a supplier would mean that he will never invoice again next week, next month, or next year for the same order.

Everything has been closed. The statement of account, which is attached to it, can testify that he got paid for all the invoices and there is no more invoice. It's all completed. So this safeguard you against that risk of receiving a late invoice later on, you did not expect it to and you receive a late invoice. So have you done a PO Close Out Signed by the supplier and Stamped? If you have done it, you can show to suppliers this has been stamped signed by you officially last year, last month. Now, I'm not going to entertain your invoice request anymore. OK, so this is the main purpose for your close out letter, which I will show you in some format here.

Have Contract In Place For Customs Clearance & Shipping

Hi there ! So the first tip that you need basically to have a very good expediting and save a lot of money and hassle is to have separately, (as an option) a contract for customs clearance, because those are specialized companies and it's easy to to implement and a contract, on the other side, for freight forwarding activities.

It could be sea freight, airfreight or we are going to have the rates of the sea freight, airfreight, road freight, all this in a contract for freight forwarding and again, a separate contract (optionally) for customs clearance. All right.

And if you have these two, you need to do the work only one time for the contract, for the whole duration of the project for one year or two years or three years, whatever. And you will be able to save, again, a lot of money in terms of coordination as well as other, as well as for shipping costs. This is a deep number one.

Clubb Shipments From Same Suppliers If Possible If No Urgency

Tip number two here, it's a basic common sense tip. If you don't have the time, please make sure that you club several shipments together in one request to your freight forwarder, so you do not send multiple requests every week to different places. You try to wait. Let's say you have one shipment ready today and then in three days you are going to expect another shipment to be ready.

So if you do have the time, you wait for that second shipment to be ready and you send both requests to your freight forwarder who will combine the shipments and he will ensure to have the most efficient shipping solution for you. He will ensure based on that clubbed shipment that he will have, for example, one boat departing in the next three days instead of having two boats two shipments done separately, which will be double cost for him and for you. So this is a very common sense rule, but you have to think about it and always request you and the user or your budget holder if he can wait for a couple of days and even accept to group the shipment because it's his own financial interest.

Clubb Shipments If Same Country/City

The tip number three is about a different version of the previous one, and it's about clubbing the shipments which are in the same city or location. OK, because you might have shipments ready at the same time, but if it is two different countries, you won't change anything, OK?

You still need to have two separate shipments of two separate costs. But if it is within the same city there, definitely you are going to save money. So please make sure that you maximize the weight and you minimize the cost by clubbing the shipments which are coming from the same location.

Below 50 Kg Always Courier Services

At the tip number three is about extremely small shipment, let's say 10, 20, twenty five up to 50 KG. OK, so the rule here is that you should contact, you know, not the usual freight forwarding company, but you should contact basically the courier services, you know, like you have DHL, FedEx, Aramex, so many of them UPS, all those companies. They are extremely efficient. For small packages, small weights only.

You don't contact them for 100KG or 200 KG, never because this is so expensive. But if you have five to 10 kg, 25KG, you will see that it is the best way. Number one, they are very fast. And number two, it would be cheaper than your normal freight forwarder which you have a contract with maybe. OK, so think about this and analyze the weight and direct your new strategy based on that analysis accordingly.

Between 50 & 100 Either Courier / Air Freight / Road Freight

The tip number five is about shipments between 50 and 100 KGs, so between 50, 100 packages, you have to go for air freight, especially if you are overseas, especially if there is an emergency. But you do not use the courier services any more, you use the air freight from your shipping companies you are dealing with usually.

And you also avoid sea freight because the freight will take much longer than the air freight. So here it is, 50 to 100 KG air freight or if it is within the same country or nearby city, obviously you are going to use a road freight instead of an air freight.

Above 100 Kg Always Sea Freight Or Road Freight Under Specific

Hi there! So the tip number six here is about extremely heavy shipment 100 KG and above, right, maybe five hundred KG right, Maybe 1000, maybe a very large volume and size of shipment. In this case, there is no question asked. You have to use the sea freighting solution. You cannot use an air freighting solution.

Why? Because it's very expensive. OK, so it all depends on the weight, the size and the urgency. Once again, if there is no urgency, you must use the sea freight solution for sure. Guaranteed ! Nothing will beat that, right? But Of course you need to have two, three, four, five, six weeks down the line considering the shipping time, especially if a shipment is coming from Asia to the US, from the US to the Middle East, etc.

So this is the solution you have envisaged. You have to envisage if you have those kinds of very heavy shipments or very big shipments in terms of volume that will not fit in an airfreight (plane) either because it is narrow. OK, so you have to consider all these parameters when you make the decision.

Always Coordinate In A Single Mail With Freight Forwarder- Supplier - End

The tip number seven here, is about coordination with all stakeholders. And this is key, OK, because if you do not coordinate properly, your shipment will get delayed. You may have penalties with your customers, you may have additional cost of storage with the supplier, cost of storage with the freight forwarder,demurrage charges. So the coordination has to be very smooth here.

You cannot afford any hiccups. So what does it mean? It means that you will not necessarily have separate emails, separate calls with everybody, but everybody must be in the loop in the same email, right. So you have one email with all the information related to the shipment. You should have the supplier. You should have the freight forwarder.

You should have a logistic person /professional if there is one in your company or an expediting person, if it is not yourself, OK, you should also have the end user. So he's aware of when it is coming, what is coming in, which way it is coming. All this. OK, so please have a single trail of email with all the parties involved in the loop. It will save you time and money, believe me.

Use A Srn For Tracking, Decision Of Mode Of Shipment And To Avoid

The tip number eight is what you saw before, is to ensure that all your import shipments are coming with a Shipping Release Notes SRN, to track it, as well as to control it, control the collection, control the documentation.

This is key and I've seen some projects fail, people complaining about additional costs at the customs because of the additional cost, because the material has to be sent back. Delays because this was not implemented. So this is the best thing I'm going to tell you today. You have to use the SRN.

Please make sure about that. And you will see quickly that this will make a difference to your professionalism and to your efficiency as an expeditor. Believe me.

Certified Lean Management Professional

Lean management and Six Sigma are the most sought after business excellence strategies among the leading and progressive MNCs. Demand for certified professionals in these fields is tremendous in the global market.

This Book is prepared with a view to provide the complete learning of Lean management, Only one of its kinds of philosophy, processes, tools and techniques followed by Toyota to manufacture its cars.

Lean management is an essential part of lean thinking. It is all about customer focus, developing and maintaining systems and processes to provide value as defined by its customers.

Who this Book is for

1. Business managers, entrepreneurs, quality consultants, doctors, research scholars, engineering and management students.
2. This is a must do Book for those who have undergone six sigma green or black belt training.

Welcome to the Mind-Blowing Book on Lean Six Sigma

Hi there, this is truly the organization here. Welcome to this ultimate Book on INSIGHT to post pandemic importance of Lean Six Sigma. This Book contains some amazing, valuable lessons. I'm going to give a complete introduction right now in my own aspect in terms of what all this. Topics that are taught in the Book are about.

So let's talk a bit about Six Sigma since its introduction as a corporate strategy by Jack Welch at General Electric in 1995. Six Sigma has come a very long way since then. It has been widely adopted in a variety of industries. The Greek letter Sigma is used to represent the variation in the process. And we all know that Six Sigma is usually defined as a fact based, data driven philosophy of improvement that favors defect prevention or defect detection.

Six Sigma practitioners have created a variety of methodologies over the years to make the approach to these initiatives consistent and driven by tactics that have been proven successful over time. Six Sigma aspires us to do the following. In general. Did you mind a problem? Gather information about the problems, according to process, develop prospective Problem-Solving data driven solutions to determine the best alternative. Put the solutions to the test.

Create a system that will allow you to maintain a long term solution and analyze the data and make any necessary adjustments. Let's get down to what this online Book covers. This Book teaches you the fundamentals of Six Sigma. It not just helps with change management within your company, but also helps your organization to prepare for the new normal. Customer expectations or demands are constantly changing in this world governed by technology.

Six Sigma has emphasis on customer satisfaction, enables the company to produce higher quality products and increase customer loyalty over time. A product focused strategy compares the product, the products of competitors in order to reach or slightly exceed such levels. You must know that Six Sigma focuses on minimizing price variation and improving process control in the process. Whereas lean and courageous work, standardization and flow by eliminating waste, which is non-value added processes and procedures.

Please note that to achieve success, leveraging the Six Sigma methodology, organizational processes must have a failure rate of no more than three point four per million, ninety nine point nine nine nine six six percent eight tenses. A Six Sigma defect is anything that isn't according to the client's specifications. Its goal is to reduce the amount of variation in commercial and production operations. The capacity to focus on producing quantitative and measurable financial gains from any Six Sigma project is one of the most notable features.

Employees can identify problem areas as well as reoccurring difficulties that affect the overall quality expectation of a service or product from a customer's perspective using Six Sigma methodology. Why offer this Book a proven game changer by completing this Lean Six Sigma White Belt online Book? You will gain the basic understanding of what Lean Six Sigma is and how Lean Six Sigma brings a plethora of benefits to your organization. If you are a professional individual who wants to grow and sustain in this ever changing competitive world, where speed is no longer just a good to have criteria and want to discover a way to fit in the new norms with their employees, then this Book is for you to learn and master this mind blowing Book.

They'll walk you through unbelievable insights and learning that you don't want to miss at all as a newbie entering the world of Lean Six Sigma. And what's more, we will teach you the five core skills of Lean Six Sigma that can be leveraged for individuals. We will also showcase a Lean Six Sigma organizational structure for better understanding of the concept topic. Other than that, we will discuss a salary range in general on various Lean Six Sigma belts. These concepts will serve to be very interesting for you all. All you need is passion and interest to learn and master this Book. There is no kind of prerequisite whatsoever. So Androulla, my lead style learning nerd, has no time to wait at all.

Introduction

I will come to these sessions. In this session, we will discuss the topic insight to post pen name importance of Lean Six Sigma. Now, as we know, organizations are facing the challenges of COVID 19. So how Lean Six Sigma can actually help organizations to weather through the current challenges. This is the focus of this session.

We are going to discuss how Lean Six Sigma can help organizations to read it through their current challenges. Now, I put together three topics for us to discuss throughout this session. First of all we will discuss the fight and abuse within Six Sigma, how Lean Six Sigma can help organizations to weather through the current challenges. And what are the challenges that the organization is actually facing right now? Where should the organization focus to change? Secondly, we will discuss Lean Six Sigma as a business process improvement methodology and business performance improvement methodology. What are some of the philosophies and the toolbox in Lean Six Sigma?

And lastly, I will discuss with you how the Six Sigma can and what did Six Sigma can actually bring to you as a professional. So do stay with me to the end of the sessions so that I can discuss with you why it is important for you as a professional to consider, to get yourself certified at the deans as the leading Six Sigma greenbelts of Black Belt. Now, this is especially true at this point in time, because Lean Six Sigma, the skills that you gained from Lean Six Sigma can actually help you to add value to your organization, beat current organizations or your future career. So stay with me at the end of these sessions. All right. So let's start to stand. Interview the topics of Fine and Oblo Lean Six Sigma right now.

Now, let's look into this survey published by McKinsey and Company back in December two or two, which is talking about Savvis actually focusing and answering the questions and how organizations can prepare for the next normal. Now, I struck a few important points from the survey, which I find is highly relevant to the data to learn Six Sigma and how Lean Six Sigma can actually help organizations in the street area. First of all, it was about setting and enforcing what boundary that means. In a way, you start to look into your work processes. And what are some of where you should really focus more and channel more resources into bear. And one of some of the areas where you should consider reducing it or even eliminating it totally so that you can actually focus your resources into what is really important to the customer and what is really important to the organizations.

Now, the next one is. I think as pointed out by this survey, that organizations should start to help people to see that it is the time for us to think about. Change. Think about what else can be changed. How can we revise our processes? How can we do something differently? Now, I'm sure you heard a saying that if you keep doing what you did in the past, you will keep getting what you get today. So in order to get the different results, organizations have to read as Zameen how they run the business, how they run the operations.

In order to face the future challenges and also coming out and facing the next normal, it becomes very, very important. So when you think about this, that means organizations actually need to. Train the people in the organizations or start to look for professionals who can help them reexamine the work processes, infect me and work as a consultant. I actually see a demand such right in many organizations coming to me and seeking help to see how I can help them to eliminate or to sultans the lead time for them to deliver the products or to look into how we can help them to improve their productivity. This is especially true where many organizations do have their work force work from remote.

Now, that talent is when people are working remotely because people suddenly do not know how to walk. Process has to flow and productivity being a. So this is the time where organizations start to look into changing the current practices. Now, last but not least, prioritize the work. We have to really prioritize what is needed and what is not needed. It doesn't mean that it means to be gone the whole day, so long as people are working and people seem to be busy, then it is OK. No, no more. All right. We have to get rid of sheer busyness. Now, business does not mean we are producing results. So how did the Worx months?

By changing our processes so that we can focus on what is almost most important to the customer. So what are the expectations of the customers? How has the customer expectation changed? I believe so. Do you think so? We don't, we don't. The effects or the influence from the COVID 19, I think customer expectations are always changing and are always racing. So let's look at this, some of the three important factors in terms of customer expectations. First of all, in the low cost, which directions do you think the customer is expecting it to be higher or lower? I think we all know the answer is, Of course, the customer is expecting a lower cost. Castable is always coming back to the organization and saying, how can you reduce the cost to me? So organizations have to find a way to save the cost and in order to do that. Organizations need to find ways to eliminate unnecessary waste.

And what about internal quality? Is it higher or lower? And Of course, we all know that the expectations of quality of product or quality of service is getting higher and higher. Customers are expecting better quality at a lower cost. And what about internally the speed of delivery faster? So if you look at this as a not so customer, always expect better quality, faster delivery and a lower cost. So if we are not able to meet this, then we are facing the challenges of losing a customer and hence losing our business. In order to do this.

Organizations need to find a way to improve productivity. How can I give to the customer what they want at the right cost with the right quality when they need it? This becomes one of the most important challenges. So the question is how to go about doing this.

Five Enablers with Lean Six Sigma for Organizations

Let's look into that message. Look into how Lean Six Sigma can help organizations to reduce the cost, improve the level of quality of products or services, and improve the speed of the delivery. Now, if you look at organizations of business performance, if you look at this symbol like a hot to have for every business, even I say the hot soup manufacturing sectors will be the operations that end to end operations. And what I mean by end to end operation is from the point you received, the order you produce it and you ship it to the customer. That is the heart of the whole operation.

And if you look at the service industry, the heart of the operation is the service operations from the customer walking to your shop, according to your calls. And Bill, until you deliver the service and make your customers happy with the service. Those are the heart of their operations. Your costs, your quality, your speed of delivery. They are all lying inside the heart of your operations. So in order to keep the customer happy and the organization healthy, the most important thing is to keep this heart healthy. So there are Fight and Able's that Lean Six Sigma can do. First of all, Lean Six Sigma is a good methodology that helps you to shorten the end to end times deliberately.

I mean, instead of you taking 30 days or 60 days to deliver the order to the customer, can you shorten it to 30 days? Can you shop in these two? In this, I recently had customers come back to me because one of their customers wanted to load a huge order for them. And the conditions that the customer gave to them is that you need to deliver to me in two months time instead of three months, which is the current performance. So they are under the pressure to reduce the lead time by at least one month from what they are able to do today. So Lean Six Sigma is one of the good two that can help you to reduce the speed of your to increase the speed of your process and reduce the cycle times of the process.

We're going to discuss this in much more detail in the next few weeks. You know, the second thing is Lean Six Sigma is here to help you to improve your productivity. And what I mean by productivity, that means you can do more with the same resources. How can you achieve more with the same resources that you have today or even be the last resources that you are having? Can you produce more? Now, the third one is in terms of quality. Lean Six Sigma is a good tool that helps organizations to raise the quality to the Six Sigma level of quality and what do I mean by Six Sigma level quality, Six Sigma level quantities, talking about three point four DPB. That means I'll have one medium pot that you produce.

You can have the quality level so good that you can only produce three point four defects of one million pops that you receive. So if you are able to achieve this, it obviously helps to improve the satisfaction of your customer. And at the same time, it also helps you to reduce the cost of poor quality. And the other one is called profitability. That means it helps. So Six Sigma, when you are able to help me to improve the speed and improve, raise your productivity, improve the quality level, and therefore it definitely helps you to improve the profitability.

And what they can do is to help you to analyze your process, identify ways that Israel, where things always stuck there or where the areas where you see that are really not adding value. And yids, there are so many resources tied up into that particular process.

So how can you eliminate that kind of process or how can you make the process much more efficient so that you can free up some resources and channel resources into where it's needed? And that's definitely helped a lot in terms of improving the profitability of the organizations. Now, in order to do this for speed, productivity, quality and profitability, in short, like SPQR, P. Organizations need to look at the process. You see. Every organization has a process. You have the process of receiving the ORDELL, the process of processing the order.

The process of making the printout, debriefing the putdowns, even the process of collecting the payments from the customizer. So when there is a process means there is a chance, an opportunity for organizations to look into this process. And how can we improve it? The process. So these are the five things, a fight, a real spread. Lean Six Sigma can help organizations. And think about this. If an organization is able to improve the speed, productivity, quality and profitability and connect the process well, connect the process to Gandel. What happens to them? Other operations, you're going to be much more sensitive to the cost is definitely going to be reduced and the quality going to improve, the speed is going to improve, the productivity is going to improve.

A special note on SPQP Prediction

So now let's discuss this when we talk about speed. What did you mean by speed? No, I think there are few important areas. First of all let's look into the time to market. Now, it is very important for organizations to find a way to shorten the time to launch a new product. You cannot take the, you know, Nasri time to launch a product because things change very fast and the life cycles of the product become shorter and shorter. So if you are able to shorten the time to markets, that means additional profits and additional press cash and additional market share, Judy, organizations. And the second thing is the order to cast.

Now I see organizations where sometimes they face challenges, where they actually have a lot of order. But the challenges, they do not have capability to deliver the order on time to the customer or the time cycle time or the total lead time to deliver the order to the customer is way too low. When the lead time for you to deliver the order is too long. That actually means it takes longer for an organization to collect the cast. So the ability of the organization to shoppers this total time from order to cast becomes one of the very crucial survival factors. One of the very crucial facts of organization is to do well and to continuously stay competitive in today's business environments.

And, Of course, when we come to the Soviets as a smell. How fast can you deliver your service? If you are running a call center, can all of them say no, providing some technical support to your customer? Are you able to resolve the technical issue by your customer in just one call? Right. How fast can you resolve the issue or can you deliver the service to the customer, become one of the very important things? Now, as a matter of fact, IBM actually conducted research just last year and won. A very interesting finding by this research is that fifty five percent of organizations make permanent changes to the organization's strategy to catch up to the new norm, utilizing their existing resources to do what?

To expedite output delivery. So the very first important thing for an organization to look at is how can I shotgun my deliberate little. So that is talking about spin, then the next one is talking about productivity, which is talking about how you produce more with the same resources. Organizations are probably, you know, facing the challenge where we cannot just continuously hire to come in in order for us to fulfill the order, because bringing more hate can mean more cost and not only headcount, productivity also includes space. You know, how well and how effectively are you utilizing the space?

How well and how effectively are you utilizing the machines and equipment that you have? So how can you produce more with the same resources, becoming one of the very, very crucial factors. And in order to improve the productivity of organizations, organizations need to look into ways to simplify and streamline processes. Now, as the consultants, a lot of times I won't read organizations, and we don't feel when you first look into the whole process, as you always find an opportunity to cut short, to streamline certain processes, that sometimes these processes are kind of like inherence from the old processes. So certain steps added in due to the old practices when technology is not that advanced yet. But to date, with the advancements of technology, the advancement of digitalisation, there are many tools that can help us do things in a much more effective way.

So if we can, you know, complete a task we just took Pleck, why do we still stay and do the job in five, 10 steps? So how can we continuously eliminate or reduce and streamline the process that becomes one of the very important things for us to do? Took is, Of course, internal of quality. Now, in terms of quality, I think the very important thing is how to reduce the cost of quality. The cost of quality, a lot of time is actually hidden costs. You know, when we have a rejection, organizations have to go through, we will be scrapped. And those are actually unnecessary costs of poor quality. You know, over time probably have to be carried out because the quality is bad and the UT is low.

So therefore, in order to meet the quantity required by the customer, you know, additional productions they require in order to produce what is needed by the customer. So those are all the hidden costs of poor quality. So we need to look into ways to reduce these costs of poor quality. And the second thing is about building quality into the process. You know, I always believe that quality doesn't come through inspections. If you find that your organization is still relying on inspections to get the quantity right, then it is time to change. How do you build quality into every single process so that everyone is able to do the job right from the first time? Anyone who performs the job, they need to know what the expectations are.

What do I have to do? What is the level of quality, the standard, the quiet ones that I had to meet before I passed my work to the next process. So it's very important to build this quality mindset into every single one in the whole end to end operation process. And it's very important also when we come to building quality into the process, is to be able to identify the source of variations, one, on some of the factors that can affect the quality of performance. And the next one is, Of course, talking about the profitability, so which is very Bollen is focused in eliminating the non-value added activities, such as like unnecessary Wolfman's of the material or unnecessary waiting time that is wasted to wait for the material arrival or waiting for certain informations to be passed on to the person so that the person can carry out a job.

The time wasted in waiting for the people, waiting for information, waiting for the material. These are all in limbo and non-value added activity that organizations should know how to identify and how to eliminate that. In Lynn, we took about seven types of waste transportation: waste, inventory, waste, motion, waste weighting waste, overproduction, waste over processing waste and defects. If you know, if you ask the professionals and you are trained and you know how to go in and identify the seven waste. You have a lot of value to your organizations because each waste that you eliminate means additional profits to the organizations. So that is what I mean by eliminating the unnecessary waste.

More About Lean Six Sigma and how it is an Evolution

So what does Lean Six Sigma know that we know in order for organizations to continuously stay competitive and do well and live, you know, do better in the next new normal? Organizations need to do folding, improve the speed, productivity, quality and profitability. And in order to do this organization, you need to look into the processes, how they can be connected to processes better together. So what is Lean Six Sigma? So Lean Six Sigma is actually a management driven scientific methodology.

And it is a very proven metallurgy for product and process improvement, which can create a breakthrough in financial performance and customer satisfaction, especially in this area of speak up. Now, Lean is a very powerful tool. Originally evolved from the Toyota production system. And it is a tool of philosophy that can help us to look into eliminating the waste. Whereas Six Sigma is focusing on reducing the variations. And what do we mean by variations? Just think about this. If you go to a cafe and you order a cup of cappuccino and it tastes so good, and if you come back to that same cafe and you order another cup of captured cup of tea, you know, if the taste came like run up the Lord, then there is a variation, then customer wouldn't like it.

Reducing variation actually means your ability to produce the product by different people, able to produce the product in the same level quantity. That means if you get two people to do the same work, they are able to produce the same result and almost the same time. By using the same resources. If your process is stable means you are able to do that when your process is stable. I mean, you are able to get two different people to produce the same work, getting the same result, running the same processes. Whereas, on the other hand, when you have high variations, that means your quality is not stable.

To date, your quality is good to lower your quality, is that right? Still inconsistent, various and will affect your productivity, affect your quality, and hence affect the profitability and will slow down the process cycle times or lead time as a whole. So let's look into, you know, Lean Six Sigma, how it can actually benefit the end to end process. If you look at this process, flow is kind of like the end to end process. Every type of industry, any type of organization, is at a very high level. The process more or less looks like this. You will start identifying what the customer won and then we'll go into the product development.

And that's where we were designing the service of the products. And this is where the sales come in, the marketing comes in to get an order from a customer and then you are able to produce it or in internal service, you deliver the service and then you produce it and you need to ship it to the customer and you make sure the customer is happy. And then you can only collect the payment from the cons.. So the time. From the point you collect the customer to the point you collect, the cash becomes one of the crucial things that the organization has to consistently review these processes. Because from this point, gather all to collect payment. These are where most of the resources are loaded in. And if you can shop this lead time, that means you are shortening the time for you to collect the cast.

So how can Lean Six Sigma help me? For example, learn to actually look into your work processes and take this approach and how do you eliminate waste throughout the processes? So you, first of all, look at your end to end process and identify where the area is. You can simplify the process. Where is the area? You can eliminate some non-value added tasks in a process and make it lead, reducing the waste. And once you do that, once you simplify it, the next thing is how do you reduce the variations in other things, make your process more stable so that your process is able to consistently produce what the customer wants at the consistent level of quality with the lower cost and the faster delivery times. So Lean and Six Sigma won't be as good as two twin brothers or three twin sisters.

All right. So lean focused in eliminating waste and Six Sigma focus in reducing the variations. So one is making the process stable. One is making the process run faster. So if the merit of this to become one of the very, very powerful tools. So what are some of the toolbox, if you look at the Lean Six Sigma metallurgy and the lean focus in identifying the waste, eliminating the waste and validating the results, and Of course, when you go through the Lean Six Sigma Green Belt or black belt training, and that is where you're going to learn some of the lean toolbox, for example, the Richel management's planning. How do you design your process so that your process is able to meet the demand from your customer?

How do you set the pace of the process so that you know how you can design your process to make sure your process continuously flows? How do you do a pool system? You create a COMBEN system in your in your in your process so that you don't end up keeping too high inventory. So lean is very, very good. And also the concept of judoka, that means build quality into your process. The concept that you built is autonomous, where the machines, for example, will be able to stop producing defects when there is something to go wrong. So what do you do? And on methods, pop. Karaoke is that. So these are some of the tools that you will learn when you roll yourself into the greenbelts and the low levels. And when we look at Six Sigma, like we sit, just know Six Sigma is focusing on reducing the process variations.

So the key thing is, first of all, we go in and identify the sources of variation where this was the area or what are the key factors that caused the process to be not stable. And Of course, by identifying the source of variations, we will be able to reduce the variations. And Of course, there are tools that help us to validate the results. So in the Six Sigma toolbox, when you open the two boxes, you'll have methods on how to do problem solving, the root cause analysis and also data. I think data is one of the very, very important pieces of information that an organization has lots of data about. Sometimes an organization doesn't make full use of the data from the process to make a wise decision.

You know, the data collected from the process can help you to understand the characteristics of your process, and hence, you know, the behavior of your process, and hence you will be able to tweak the process. So then the process can become more stable and can run at a higher and a faster speed and more consistent quality performance. So, Of course, in Minsk in Six Sigma April, we will learn some statistical tools which can help you to analyze your process and do some regressions of forecasts from your process data to do some predictions so that you can predict the behavior, the performance of the process. Right.

You can even do the experiment of designing the design of experiments to optimize the parameters of your process. So these are all very important skill sets. And a combination of Lean Six Sigma gives you this comprehensive toolbox that enables you to at any one time pull out the right to to improve the performance of your process. So Lean Six Sigma methodology, follow what I call it, Dybek, Jan, Bitcoin, Demet DME, I see Mr. thoBe define we define the problem and then we use some with two to marshals' day to day performance baseline so that we know where we are before we look into how to improve it. So measuring that to date performance and then analyzing the root cause and finding ways to improve the process performance and then using some tool to make sure the process is able to sustain at the new level of improved level performance. So this is a very systematic process improvement. Metallurgic DME, I see.

Give you a very systematic approach to tackle any problem with regard to the performance of your processes. So let's look into one of the two. For example, you can actually use process mapping and go in and analyze where are the areas that you can identify opportunities around an area that you see, you know, or, you know, a lot of times when we deal with a cross-functional team. Sometimes there are cross-functional gaps, which we need to address so that the process can run smoothly. So by using the process, which is one of the tools in site Lean Six Sigma, it helps you to analyze your process and identify where the point of disconnect is.

Where is the point where it is very critical to achieve the level of performance that you want in that process? And this is just another example, when you look at the whole process and you start to identify where the value is and based on the value added. So by taking this approach based on my experience, we can always find opportunities to achieve these 20 to 30 percent improvement in productivity. Right. In your overall process performance. And when you eliminate those in recolor, unnecessary, non-value added, you can actually saltines the lead time of your whole process performance.

So this is how powerful the Lean Six Sigma can actually help you to do. So where do we apply the Six Sigma, Lean Six Sigma applications into which industry, which kind of industry? All right. So, Of course, the original focus of Lean Six Sigma is very much into the manufacturing cycle. But I think today, even the nonmanufacturing sector will start to actually adopt Lean Six Sigma. And it is equally applicable to both the manufacturing and nonmanufacturing sectors. To me is anywhere where there is a process that is a waste. And that means, in other words, wherever there is a process, Lean Six Sigma can be there to help organizations, to eliminate waste and make the process more stable.

So the manufacturing sector can be automotive industry, heavy industry, micro assembly or medium enterprise industry. So it can be applied across quite a wide range of industries. When you look into the non manufacturing sector, I think today now even some health care Sentell or healthcare industry hospitals, for example, are adopting the Lean Six Sigma approach, finance industry now banking, who is actually hiring Lean Six Sigma, Green Belt or Black Belt S.M., as well as education cycles and even military defense sector. They are all requiring Lean Six Sigma.

Five Core Skills with Lean Six Sigma

So that is pretty much about how Lean Six Sigma can help the organizations in SPQR, the full area, and also connecting the process and what is Lean Six Sigma? By now, you understand Lean is helping the organization to eliminate waste. Six Sigma helps the organization to stabilize the process, reduce the variation. So what is in it for you as a professional? Now there are more than coal steels that you can acquire by going through the Lean Six Sigma certifications.

And one of the five, let's look at them one by one. First of all, graphical techniques by going to learn Six Sigma curriculums. By signing up for the Lean Six Sigma green greenbelts or black belt certifications, you will learn a couple of techniques to turn data into useful graphical techniques. Now, some are not. And the picture tells a thousand words. So if you are able to use graphical techniques like histogram box plot control charts and Run charts and things like that, you can actually present your data in a much more effective way. So one of the skills is to acquire graphical techniques.

The second one is the ability to analyze the data. I think this scale has become even more important as the industry as a whole is moving to what industry 4.0, the data become very, very crucial. So statistical analysis, the tool that you will learn in the Lean Six Sigma certification program, gives you some basics, as well as some abun statistical analysis tools that help you to become better as a data scientist, for example. Right. You know how to analyze the process and how to analyze the data and turn the data into useful information so that organizations can make the right decisions at the right time.

And Of course, as a certified Lean Six Sigma Green Belt and Black Belt, you become very good at analyzing the process. You look into the process, you know, way to identify the critical bottleneck, you know, where to attack. She needed to shorten the cycle time, you know, when to attack in order to raise the productivity of the whole process. Baphomet, you know, where to attack in order to reduce the cost. So you become very good at analyzing the process. And this is one of the very crucial skills that is highly demanded. Then the next one is business process management. You know, the six o'clock approach I see and analyze the process. You become a battle in managing the process.

You know where to go. Highlight a way to manage the AYRO, which is the either Erio process, which is almost important to the customer. So you know how to design the process so that the organization can deliver what the customer won when they want it and the right quality with the right quantity. So you become a battle in business process management. And last but not least, you are trained to be more systematic and structured. No Lean Six Sigma training helps you to look at things in a systematic way. Right. So you know how to take the approach where you will be able to look at the current performance and deep dive into identifying the root cause. Coming up, the Bill of Rights Solutions testing whether to see the solution is effective or not put in the right to to make sure the process is sustainable. So these are the five essential skills that if you become very good at this, I am sure it helps you to add a lot of weight to your risk.

To me and a lot of weight to your value that you can't add to the organization is not just about the certificates that are certified as greenbelts or black belt. I think it's more important that this decertifying skills, if you have this fine skill, most organization need you because anyone with this fine skill, that means this person is able to help the organization, to reduce the cost, to improve the productivity, to improve the profitability, to improve the speed of the process. So, no, just a very overview of different levels about levels. Of course, at very fundamental levels, we look at that yellow belt, these and Modula, and these are the people who understand basic Hoplin, Six Sigma.

They are trained with some basic tools that they can do some simple, simple improvement or in Bitcoin, Kysen, improvement within the organization. So usually the line works. For example, you can train some of the technicians and some of your operators even to be certified as yellow belt so that they all have some basic improvement to azonto. They know how to recognize the seven weeks. So these are the people who can drive and the day to day meeting, meaning improvement within the organizations, then at the next level is called greenbelts.

Now, this is the individual who has already acquired some important skill sets from lean to both, as well as from six to box. So these are the people who can actually lead or support projects or in fact, for many of you, I would if you have not got yourself certified as their belts. If you are a good looking engineer in any organization, I strongly encourage you to look into and throw yourself into one of our upcoming programs of Lean Six Sigma certified Lean Six Sigma Green Belt in September. Now, if you want to move up to the level, the next level black belt Noveck Belt is usually the person who is involved in leading or inculcating the Lean Six Sigma culture in the whole organization.

So Black Belt is also the person who can actually manage multiple projects, multiple Greenmount projects. So that is the next level. And Of course, the next level will be the muscle black belt, which you become to coach the consultants and also you become the person or the sitting in the community. The chairman is leading the Lean Six Sigma community. All right. Now, how Lean Six Sigma can help you. Well, if you look at this research that I find, I think generally in terms of the compensation on the salary comparisons in US dollar per year, like Black Belt is close to 100000 US dollar per year in one of the annual salaries and Grimble is at sixty thousand.

But, you know, just show me I got my black belt certifications back 20 years ago when I got this. And even up to today, 20 years, I'm still using the skill sets that I learned 20 years ago. And it's just because of that skill set. It helped me to move my career very fast from engineer to a manager, senior manager, directors, and today become a consultant and consistently still using this skill set to help organizations to improve the performance of Sobhan, their lead time. And I still really, really enjoy using this skill because it's like to me, it's just like, you know, like a doctor, right where I'm using this skill.

And I go into the organizations and they tell me that they have a cost problem there, poor delivery problem. They have a lead time problem. And I look into their process and I point to them, where is the area of opportunity? And we work together with them, produce it, and we see the productivity improvement, 30 percent cycle time reductions of 40 percent. And that is the joy. The satisfactions. Right. So this is why I am still very passionate about Lean Six Sigma and why I encourage all of you to really consider and join us in our Lean Six Sigma training. Now, it still has the whole coming to the end of this journey and just kind of summarizes to you as a Lean Six Sigma.

So a focus in four areas in Danoff speed. So you focus on four areas: internal speed. It gives you the ability to improve your false sense so that you can move if you can make fast and precise decisions. So you can act fast to ever changing environments and sustain the change. So one area is improving the speed. And the second area is improving productivity, which is much more effective utilization of space, for example, and also cultivating teamwork and being able to produce more by using the same resources or even less resources.

Instead of doing trees that used to snap, instead of doing fires that do two clicks. So, you know, Lean Six Sigma helps you to engage your workforce. And everybody comes forward and thinks about how I can streamline my processes? How can I make my processes become much better? So in other words, it indirectly or directly helps you to improve the productivity of your processes and then quality it, help you to improve the quality, minimize the error, and the resources are spent on the value added tasks and also intent of improving the productivity and the profitability as a whole.

All right. See, kind of like when you're able to improve the speed, the productivity, the quality, your profitability becomes much better. So your resources are spent wisely in the right area. And every single resource you spend is producing positive results and the right profitability for your organizations.

Customer Service to Customer Relationship Management

While all businesses focus their efforts on excellent customer service it usually ends there. It is also important that the relationship built with the customer from the point of sale is sustained. The goal of your business should be to develop brand ambassadors and it starts with your regular customers! This Book is designed for the learner to understand and acknowledge their role in the development of a culture of Service. It is expected that the learner will have a clear understanding of their role in customer relationships and learn skills in handling difficult situations with ease so as to project a positive and professional image of the business to its customer.

Introduction

Hello there. My name is Andy Hanselman, who is Andy Hanselman? While I help businesses, their leaders, their people think in three D, which is about being dramatically and demonstrably different. I work around the world speaking, training and consulting. I've written a book all about three D businesses, and this Book is all about addressing some of the key challenges that businesses have today because these challenges have never been bigger.

We're in a fast moving and ever changing world, ever more competitive markets, massive customer choice, increasing customer and employee expectations and in lots of cases, tightening budgets, all exasperated by what we call a CCTV world, a world of never ending change, of ever increasing connectivity and greater and greater transparency. And it's all happening with such velocity.

It all makes things much more difficult for today's businesses and a different approach is needed, a dramatically and demonstrably different approach. We've even researched, worked with, trained and learned from these businesses. We call them three D businesses and what you're going to learn in this Book is how to forget CRM and think MKR.

That means maximizing your customer relationships, how three D businesses maximize their relationships and creates unsurpassable levels of customer loyalty, repeat business and increase profitability while you and your business should be doing it too. How you can take a dramatically and demonstrably different approach to maximizing your customer relationships. And we're going to share with you some of the common reasons why businesses fail to do it effectively.

See how you measure up and identify ways that you can overcome these barriers in your business or in your team. It's how to develop a proactive approach to maximum relationships with the customers. You want to do more business with them and create practical, cost effective ideas and steps to help you do it. We'll give you the tools and techniques to develop your own maximizing customer relationship plan that actually delivers.

So by the end of this Book, you will know how to get closer to and build stronger, more profitable relationships with your customers. Identify and establish who those customers actually are. We're going to help you improve your levels of repeat business referrals and your profitability and help you look at how you can prioritize your time, resources and efforts on the right customers to make that happen.

You'll learn how to take a proactive approach to making it happen in your business and take the steps to create a maximized customer relationship plan that you make happen in your business. I just like to stress there'll be no academic theories or magical answers. Are there any? There will be real practical examples of businesses who have done this and are doing it tools and techniques that you can actually develop and use in your business.

You'll also get some toolkits and templates that you can download and use to make it all work for you. So let's get started and maximize those customer relationships.

What It Is And What It Isn't

Let's start with maximizing customer relationships. What's all that about? Well, I'll start with a question. What do Spotify, Amazon Go and my local pub have in common? They all know and understand their customers and deliver a great personalized experience as a result. Spotify sent me an email recently with a time capsule playlist with my most listened to tracks in the past 12 months.

What it was, who it was by the genres of music, how often I listened, but also some of the new music I'd listened to. I might have forgotten about it. And there are some wonderful recommendations and track listings for me to consider based on this. Some absolutely brilliant stuff. Although it was very personal, it didn't seem too intrusive. It's clear that they know I'm an aging rocker that maybe needs to get into today's modern world, but also likes listening to new music as well.

And they've demonstrated they care about me by making some great recommendations. Amazon Go is a store in Seattle where you walk into the store, and as long as you've got your iPhone on you, you get your crisps, you get your sandwich, you get your drinks, you walk out again and they just invoice you. They know what you've bought. And they'll make recommendations to tell you when they've got special offers on Emma, the landlady at the Beehive Pub in Harthill in South Yorkshire knows I like Red Feather beer and is ready to greet me with a freshly poured pint as I occasionally walk into the pub.

The result is happy and devoted customers who get what they want. They're happy to come back for more and they're happy to tell other people. That's a maximized relationship. Lots of business leaders tell me they've actually got a CRM focus. They've invested in fantastic IT systems, they've trained everybody. They've spent a fortune. They're ready to take on the world. The reality is it's a database with lots of names on it, often spelt wrong. There's an emphasis on form filling.

And in a world where maintaining and keeping customers is becoming ever more difficult, I'm afraid this just doesn't work. I tell them to forget CRM and focus on MKR, which is all about maximizing customer relationships and our definition of maximizing customer relationships is this proactively developing relationships that give the best to and get the best from the customers that you want. And there are some key things here that I want you to emphasize and take on board.

The first one, the customers that you want. It's about identifying and focusing your efforts on them. The second key element of this is giving the best to them by getting close to them, understanding their wants and needs, making them feel valued through exceptional service, great responsiveness, and creating what we call the ties that bind. It's a personalized experience that demonstrates you care about them. And the third ingredient is getting the best from them in terms of ongoing loyalty, repeat business, increase sales, profits, referrals, recommendations, ideas, opinions and support. So let me just stress.

It's not about databases or customer analytics. And Of course, I'm not knocking databases or any of these things, but 3D businesses know that it's what you do with the stuff that counts. So it's not about filling forms in. It's about relationships and it's about maximizing them. Let's now look at how we can do that and why it's important for your business to have a go at this.

Why It's So Important And How So Many Businesses Get It Wrong

Why is this stuff so important? Well, are you in a world of increasing competition? Have your customers got more choice? Are you in a world where most of us are? Customer loyalty is declining. A recent study of more than 34,000 consumers worldwide by Verint systems showed that customer loyalty and retention is declining. Two thirds of customers surveyed said they are more likely to switch to the competitor. That demonstrates they care.

Customers are less forgiving. According to Accenture, 47% of consumers stop doing business with the supplier after one moment of disappointment. On the upside, if things do go wrong, according to Think Jar Research, 67% of customer churn is preventable if the issue is resolved straight away. In other words, if you're spotting disappointment and dealing with it, engaging with your customers, you can keep them. 83% of consumers say that customer experience is a major factor in staying with their service providers.

Salesforce showed that 84% of customers say being treated like a person not a number, is very important to winning and keeping their business. So what we actually start to see is that if this stuff works, you can build on it. Loyal customers, for example, do come back for more and spend more. Fundera reported that 43% of customers spend more money on brands to which they are loyal. 91% of customers are more likely to shop with brands that provide specific offers that are relevant to them.

And 31% of shoppers wish their shopping experiences were more personalized than they currently are. And what we're seeing is that this personalization is something that really, really has an impact on customers. In a study of over 100,000 customers by Matista, they identified that customers who have an emotional connection to a business have a customer lifetime value that's four times higher than the average customer. That means they stay longer and they spend more. Customer lifetime value is a way of looking at your customers. How long is a typical customer staying with you?

How long is how many pounds shillings pence do those customers actually spend with you? Multiply those things together. That actually works out what the customer lifetime value is. It's maybe helping you think about the long term picture. Research also indicates that in the UK it typically costs 6 to 10 times more to sell to a new customer than it is to an existing one. 6 to 10 times more. But so many businesses fail to actually recognize this and don't focus on building and maximizing those customer relationships.

In other words, they go chasing it, but they don't actually build on it. It all seems so obvious, doesn't it? But so many businesses get it so wrong. Are you one of those businesses? Why is this? Well, here are 12 things that we see businesses do That means they fail to maximize their customer relationships. And as we go through these, I'd like you to think about your own business and work out how you measure up. There is an assessment tool you can download to help you do this. So let's go through them and work out what this might mean for you and for your business.

One. They do nothing. There's a complete passiveness. There's reactivity and even apathy. They seem to be the key drivers in these businesses. Sometimes they're still very, very busy, but busy doing the wrong things and focusing inwards. It's often because there's no drive and direction from the top. Maybe it's because they are too busy chasing new customers and not building on the customer relationships they've actually created. In terms of building and maximizing customer relationships with the customer they've created, they're actually ignoring them. They put all the effort in and then do nothing about it.

Problem two. It's all about the data. It's never the customer. The focus is very much on filling, on filling in forms, ticking boxes, keeping the data accurate, not actually using it. Yes, information is good, but it's what you do with it that counts. The message to the customer is please just tick this box. That's what's important to us. Barrier. Three There's no buy in to this. The research suggests around 65% of CRM projects actually fail due to low user adoption. What that actually means is people don't see the relevance or the benefit to them.

The training. The support, maybe in some cases, the inclination to make it work or what I see in lots of businesses, it's on the edge. It's a department, it's somebody else's job. It's not used, it's not dated, and it's not managed. Another barrier that I sometimes see people say is, Oh, we've got a loyalty scheme that should be okay. They think it's about schemes and vouchers. I probably shouldn't tell anybody this.

If I go into a coffee retailer, Have you got a loyalty card? I get it out and show it to them. Little do they know I've got four other cards of their competitors. I'm not that loyal. According to a recent survey by KPMG, only 37% of consumers believe current loyalty programs are effective in earning their favor. They're just there. 95% of UK shoppers want brands to seek new ways to reward their loyalty. And what they say would do this is to pay attention to product quality, provide value for money and a great customer experience.

What we're saying here is don't just throw points at people to reward their loyalty. That's just a thing that goes on at the end of it. You've got to make sure you're delivering things effectively and professionally all the time. Barrier five is passiveness. There's no proactivity or there's no focus. The result is inconsistency. And customers who feel that they're not important or that you're not bothered. The Sixth Barrier, There's no strategic approach.

There are no goals. There's no plan. There are mixed messages and inconsistency. In some cases, there are no messages at all. It's about getting a clear focus. And that's what Barrier seven is, what we actually see in lots of businesses. The focus is on the wrong customers. They don't know who their best customers are. They waste lots of time, effort and money. For example, chasing the wrong ones. They don't recognise this lifetime value of a customer.

How many customers will come back at what frequency? How much will they spend in that period? What we also see within those businesses that actually sometimes focus on the wrong people, in other words, they don't recognise that within a particular business or a family, there are a number of people who make decisions. They only focus on one of them and actually ignore the others, which means that again, they're not actually getting people on board to actually make this work. Barrier eight They don't understand. They don't understand their customers' needs, their wants, their opinions, and they do very little to find out.

The result is they miss out on opportunities for more sales and to build stronger, lasting relationships. Barrier nine There is no personalization. They don't demonstrate. They understand their customers and create a bond with them. We call it the ties that bind. They actually show it to the customers. You're not just a number. We actually do care about you. So many messages that get sent out there saying you're just a number. Barrier ten. They're the same as their ongoing communication is anonymous. It's boring. It's irrelevant. They don't differentiate themselves from their competitors, and the result is a lack of trust. Anonymity. You're seen as being the same as and let's be honest, in today's competitive markets, same as sucks.

Barrier 11 Mismatches. They communicate the wrong way from the customer's point of view. They use the wrong channels, the wrong format, the wrong frequency, and the result is no engagement with their customers. And the last one is they just shout. They bombard customers with noisy, aggressive, pushy messages. The result is customers just opt out. So even if you never say it and hopefully don't mean it, the common messages to your customers from lots of lots of businesses could be We don't really care.

We're not bothered about you. We're all the same. We're more important than you. Oh, and by the way, please buy from us. We're really good. Honest. Might you be sending some messages like that to your customers? Download the assessment tool. Take some time out to review your approach and create a clear picture of how you and your business measures up. And then watch the next chapter to actually see, well, what do successful 3D businesses do to forget CRM, think MKR and maximize their customer relationships?

The 7 Key Ingredients Of Maximizing Your Customer Relationships

So what do 3D businesses do to maximize their customer relationships? I will stress again, it's not about heavy sales, pushy selling techniques, but the definition that we introduced earlier. Proactively developing relationships to give the best to and get the best from the customers you want. So how do they do it?

Well, here are some key facts for success. Things we see 3D businesses do. There is a tool kit you can download to assess yourself as we go through these and create some time just to think a bit about how you are doing these things? Are you doing them well? Could you do them better? So let's look at these seven key factors for success.

The first one, 3D Businesses think strategically and get focused. They develop a strategic view to creating, developing and maintaining win win relationships with the

customers they want to. They ensure their efforts and resources are focused on those customers and they prioritize plans to maximize those relationships and actually create the opportunities and maximize those opportunities that they provide. Are you doing that?

Key Factor two they understand what their customers think and want. They understand who their best customers are, but they also understand what they want and what a maximized relationship looks like to those customers. They get to know them. They get to know their needs, their wants, their challenges. They also understand their aspirations and what they want from suppliers. And as a result, they tailor their offer to each of those customers. And that leads us on to key factor three. They get personal.

They make their customers feel valued by personalizing their offer, their communication and their approach. They know that the more personalized it feels, the more difficult it is for competitors to get in there and to break what we call the ties that bind. Success Factor four They create dialogue, not diatribes. And they listen to their customers. They recognize that customers need to be engaged. As a result, they work hard at creating real conversations with their customers via the appropriate channels and formats and the frequency that those customers want, whether that's online or offline or both.

It's what's right for the customer. They have proactive feedback mechanisms that tell them what their customers really think about them and their performance, and they take action as a result. Success Factor five is that 3D businesses add value. They regularly and proactively provide customers with relevant new ideas and solutions that add real value. These are the things that differentiate them from their suppliers. It's about solving problems, taking away the pain. They educate their customers and support them. They do it in a timely and appropriate manner that works for the customer, not themselves.

Key success Factor six is they maximize opportunities and think about the share of customers as well as giving the best to their customers. They also focus on getting the best from them. So yes, they deliver great experiences and personalize it, but what they do is make sure they get the best from those customers in the form of repeat business, more opportunities, and loyalty. And what they do to make sure that happens is they make sure that people can spot and maximize those opportunities.

In simple terms, maximizing opportunities is the payoff and is the integral ingredient of maximizing customer relationships. No point putting all that effort in and not getting the return. So what we see 3D businesses do is proactively identify and prioritize the customers where opportunities exist and they educate them about their total capabilities. One of the things that they do is make sure that they're focusing their messages to make sure that they build and maximize their relationships And key success, Factor seven is they leverage their relationships.

They get their customers to give back, whether it's in the form of feedback, ideas, suggestions, testimonials, recommendations or referrals. They proactively encourage and sometimes incentivize their customers to give back in a value adding way. What an example of a business that actually does this particularly well. Well, yeah, I'd argue it's Amazon. First of all, Amazon is easy to buy from, although there's an incredible array of goods. The thing you actually need to find is usually relatively easy to do and it's pain free with one click. They delight you by very often delivering things quicker than they said they were going to. They personalize things.

Those emails that keep you informed of what's happening, where your delivery is, what's going on. And although it is robotic, it doesn't always appear that way. They remember you. They know what you bought last time. They educate you and make recommendations based on previous purchases. People who bought this also bought this. That creates more sales. That's the maximized bit. And they do it consistently and that's the key bit for them.

The result is a £400 billion dollar business that sets the benchmark for us all. Now, you're not Amazon. I'm not suggesting you have to copy Amazon. What I'm suggesting here is that you download them. Toolkit and assess your approach and see how you measure up against those seven ingredients. And also, while we're on this, why not see what others think? Other people in your team get their thoughts and views. And this is revolutionary stuff. Why not see what your customers think? It'll be more about that later.

Introducing The MCR Model

To explain what maximized customer relationships look like. We've put together a simple model to help you look at this in terms of your relationships. It's worth pointing out, by the way, this also applies to internal relationships, too. But one of the things you want to look at is the different types of relationships. We've actually got to explain what maximized customer relationships look like.

We've put together a very simple little model to help you look at your relationships and hopefully put this into context. And it's also worth pointing out when we start talking about this stuff, that it could also include internal customers, too. So what you'll see is a little two by two grid that looks at whether you're getting what you want from the relationship or you're not. Whether the customer is getting what they want from it or not.

And let's just take you through each of these and explain what it looks like. So the first one we're going to look at is the giving relationship. And a giving relationship is where the customer is doing very well out of this. Thank you very much. But you're not. Have you got some customers that keep coming back to you saying, can you just can you just. They're getting a great experience from you, but they're not paying you on time or they're not paying you or you're putting lots of time and effort into that particular customer and actually you're not really getting the returns that you should be looking for.

So when you start looking at this giving relationship, the customer might be very, very happy. Your challenge is to work out, is this right for us, what can we do to actually move into a maximized relationship? Because if you're not in that maximized relationship and you're in the giving relationship, if you're not careful, you'll move across what we call the losing relationship. And the losing relationship is where you're not getting what you want from it. But neither is the customer. But guess who gets blamed? Losing relationships takes a lot of energy. It Takes a lot of time.

You ever had that situation where whatever you tried to do to get out of it, it seems to cause even more and more problems. In other words, going back to the giving relationship, you need to actually draw a line in the sand and say, we're not going past that, because if you do, you'll end up in the losing relationship. The taking relationship is where you're doing very well at this. Thank you very much. But the customer isn't. And I'm not saying you shouldn't charge premium prices and do some great things to actually make sure you're making money on these things. But the taking relationship is maybe where you're not giving the real service levels that they expect.

Are you still charging them? Maybe you're in some sort of contract with them where they have to use you and you take them for granted. Taking relationships is one of the key dangers of these things is in the short term, they look great. I had a client when I was a client. A guy I met came to one of my events and he said, Oh, Andy, I've got lots of those. I charge you a fortune and I make loads of money. When we actually looked at what his business was doing, the churn was massive.

People realized what he was doing and they just moved on. He's no longer in business. So I'll stress again, I'm not saying we shouldn't make sure we get the best out of it, but we're going to make sure that customers are getting what they want from it, too.

And that leads us on to this whole idea of the maximized relationship. And the maximized relationship is where you get what you want from it and so does your customer. And that could again, work on different levels. So the maximized relationship could be, I ring you up, I ask for a price for something. You give me the price, I order it, you deliver it perfectly, you send me the invoice, I pay you. And as a transaction, that's great. But a maximized relationship might also be on. We develop things together. It's a partnership.

We invest time, money, and effort in making these things work. So what I'm suggesting here is that the maximized relationship is the goal. You get what you want from it. So does your customer. So the key thing here is to work out how your relationships measure up, look at the grid, work out which customers are where. And just a quick point here. If you've got different contacts within the same customer, particularly in a business to business situation, put the individuals in the different areas, where are they? And maybe more importantly, where is the relationship heading? So in the next chapter we're going to actually look at this in more detail. So download the toolkit, have a go at it, and let's see how you measure up.

How Do Your Relationships 'Measure Up'?

So you've downloaded the toolkit. And what we're going to do now is just give you some time to walk through this and work out where your relationships are with your customers. So use the grid and evaluate your customer relationships.

- Where are people in each box?

- Are they in a relationship?

- Are they in a giving relationship?

- Are they in the losing relationship or are they in the maximized relationship?

We're aiming to get them there. So seven questions you might want to consider to help you get the best out of this. Question one: Do you have a clear picture of what you want from your customer relationships? Have you spelled out and got a clear understanding of what a maximized relationship looks like in your business? Are all your people on board with that too? Question two Whereabouts on this grid are your key customer relationships?

Again, spend a bit of time working out and just plot them, put them on there and get a feel for where they are. Question three: How do you actually know? This just could be your opinion. So here's a little hint: Maybe you should ask your customers. Question four What can you do to find out? See the previous hint. Maybe ask your customers. Question five Which way are these relationships heading? So for each of the little dots you've put on that grid, which way is it heading?

If, for example, you're in a giving relationship, is it getting worse? Because that will actually help you identify. Question six What are you doing? What do you need to do to get them where you want them? And. Question seven What do other members of your team or business think? You might think somebody's a great customer because they buy lots from you. Your accounts department might say, Yeah, but they never pay us. So one of the things you might want to think about is what other people's thoughts and views are.

Try to start working on what this maximized customer relationship looks like. Maximizing customer relationships doesn't just happen by chance. It's a proactive process. It needs to involve everybody in your business. Yep, even your accounts department. Your challenge is to work out what maximized customer relationships means for you and what you can do to create them. It's all about creating your own recipe for success, and the following chapters will actually help you work out what that looks like and what it means for you and for your customers.

Review And Refocus Your Approach To Customers

Our experience suggests that 3D businesses have a very focused approach to identifying and targeting the customers they want to build and develop relationships with. However, so many businesses have a very scattered approach to the way they find and deal with customers, and some have no focus whatsoever. We're often told to segment our markets. How do you do that? Size, age sector, location. They're all very, very powerful ways of doing it. But here's an approach that might help you look at your approach to your potential and actual customers.

It's not set in stone, and it's aimed to maybe help create a bit of debate discussion and doing another 3D. You may see there's a theme here emerging as we do these, because what I want to give you are the ten DS of different customers. As ever, there is a toolkit you can download to take you through these. But I'm going to give you a description of each of them.

The next chapter will give you a bit of time to maybe work out what it means for you. So have a look at these and start thinking about your customers and start working out where people are in this. Maybe more importantly, what do you need to do to do something about it for your business to maximize customer relationships? So let's start with number one, disinterested customers. These are the customers that aren't interested in what you provide, and that's fine, provided Of course you can find sufficient customers that are interested.

Our definition of marketing is finding, attracting and keeping the customers that you want while maximizing your profits. 3D businesses identify and focus on the customers they want to work with. They choose them or lose them. And they're not all things to all people. As a result, they don't waste time, energy and resources on customers they don't want to work with. That could be the same for you. Stay away from them. Leave them to it. So some questions for you.

Who and where are your target customers? Are your efforts focused on them or are you wasting time, effort and resources and money and those that simply aren't interested? The second type of customer is your ideal customer. These are the ones you want. 3D businesses focus on specific customers and understand those customers, their needs, their problems and their preferences. They have proactive processes for targeting and attracting these customers and ensure the right messages get through to these customers via the channels that work for them.

They also establish a dramatic difference, which is an unmatchable bundle of products, service skills and methods and practices that differentiate the business from its competition. It's tough their competitors aren't doing or even better, stuff they can't do. Customer focused businesses recognise that their dramatic difference is only any good if their customers want it, recognise it and prepare to pay for it. Even better is to be prepared to pay more for it. So some questions for you.

• Where do your ideal customers come from?

- Who are they?

- Do you actually know who they are and what they look like?

- What do they want?

- And how can you track more of them?

The third type of customer is the detached customer. Detached customers are those that you've won. There's no real loyalty. They're reasonably happy with you. They think you're okay. They might come back. Equally, they might not. There's no real relationship or buy-in to who you are and what you're doing. And the result is you are simply seen as being the same as or just one off.

The result is customer churn and the constant fight to attract new business. Truly, customer focused businesses identify these customers and work hard to build on the relationships they've started. Crucially, they work out what they need to do to increase customer loyalty, and a good starting point is to establish what those customers think, what they need and what they want from you. Find out what you need to do to deliver this. And the challenge then is to find ways to exceed their expectations and demonstrate how much you care. So some questions for you with these types of customers.

- What are you doing to build on the hard work you've done in engaging them?

- Do they recognise your dramatic difference?

- Do you have one?

- And the next question, what can you do to create the fourth type of customer, the delighted customer?

These are the customers whose expectations you've exceeded. It means a surprising level of service you provide in a positive way. It's not about giving things away for nothing or just doing things for free. It's about the personal touch. It's making them feel valued. It's creating a wow reaction. And scarily, in some sectors, this simply means doing things on time, on budget, with a smile. It makes commercial sense that the Ipsos Loyalty report highlights that in a business to business engagement, delighted customers are five times more likely to plan on repurchasing than merely satisfied customers.

We've actually developed a Book on Expert Academy about delivering outstanding customer experiences. You might want to check that out and see how you can make this stuff work in your business. And it talks about the principles of customer delight, and the six ingredients of customer delight are producing a reaction, it appears, spontaneous or unexpected. It's the personal touch. It makes customers feel valued and it's genuine and it's memorable. It gets people talking. It's not a gimmick.

And what we actually see 3-D businesses do is they build into the way they do business and the way they do things. So some more questions for you.

- How do you delight your customers?

- What could you do to become their first choice?

- Even better, what could you do to be their only choice?

Now, the downside of customer delight is that by definition, by delivering it, you raise expectations. That's not a bad thing, but it means you've actually got to build on this stuff consistently and deliver a great experience all the time and help create the fifth type of customer. Devoted customers. Devoted customers have high expectations of you and consistently get a great experience. And it's great as judged by them. By the way, not you.

These are the customers that typically come back for more. They spend more. They tell other people. And that consistency means that there's no reason for them to go anywhere else. And what we see in three D businesses, this doesn't happen by chance. They actually make this work for them and create a culture that supports this. They get everybody involved. They build the systems and support, actually make it work, and they give their people the skills, tools and permission to deliver it.

A proactive approach to spotting and maximizing opportunities is an integral ingredient of customer focus with devoted customers. We've already outlined that by getting the best from them is what it's all about. It's the repeat business, it's the loyalty, it's the recommendations, the referral and hopefully the increased spend. But it never fails to amaze us how many businesses seem obsessed with chasing the new ones rather than putting their effort into maximizing existing ones. So you're creating these devoted customers some questions for you to work on.

- How do you create them?

- But are your systems and processes there to support and reinforce that?

- Are you building on that and are you actually maximizing those relationships?

The sixth type of customer is the disappointed customer. These are the ones that aren't happy with what you've done and what you've delivered. They've had a poor experience and the way you've done this means you've failed to meet their expectations. And again, poor is defined by them and often compared not necessarily to your competitors, but to the great experience they've had from you in the past. Three D Businesses work hard to prevent disappointment, but recognise that things do wrong even in their businesses. It's what happens next that differentiates them. They spot and deal with disappointment by proactively seeking customer feedback. They establish systems and processes and mechanisms to find out what their customers really, really think.

And they also empower their people to spot and solve problems. So some questions for you. How can you prevent disappointment in your business? But if it does happen, are your people equipped and encouraged to spot and deal with disappointment? Do they do that? Because if they don't, it will lead to the seventh type of customer that disaffected customers. These are usually the ones that are disappointed that you didn't spot them, didn't spot the issue, didn't sort it out. Not only are they the ones that are now ignoring your marketing messages and efforts, many are quite happy to spread the bad news about you both via word of mouth and word of mouth. So you put all this marketing effort into them.

It's actually being ignored because they've switched off. As we mentioned, three D businesses work hard at avoiding creating these at all times, but yet you've guessed it, dealing with disappointment does actually happen. You've got to work out how it works for you. But if they do slip through the net and things do go wrong, what do you need to do to get those customers back? And you can actually do that by spotting it, looking out for it, and ensuring that everybody in your team is focusing on these things to get everybody back on track with it.

In other words, you can still look out for and listen to disaffected customers, for example, on online forums, channels. Are you keeping an eye on what's going on? Do you have a search facility to actually make sure that you know what's going on out there and what people are saying about you? They might not tell you. They might tell other people. A recent survey. Trustpilot suggests that 89% of UK customers are influenced by negative reviews and 78% are actually deterred from making a purchase altogether.

So in other words, if you've got these disaffected customers, you've got to look out for them. You've got to find ways of maybe trying to overcompensate for that and make sure that you're dealing with these things in a professional but proactive way. How businesses actually respond to negative views, for example, is a very critical thing here. Apparently, 15% of customers say they're more likely to do business with a company after reading a response to a negative review than if it was resolved. In other words, it's not just about dealing with disappointment.

It's about being seen to be dealing with it. So guess what? Some more questions for you. What are you doing to spot and listen to disaffected customers? What do you do to demonstrate you're actually dealing with them? The eighth type of customer is the dormant customer. These are the customers who don't currently buy from you but have them in the past. And these are a massive potential opportunity, provided, Of course, they're not disaffected. They well, well have thought that you were good at the time and whatever you were doing was fantastic. But for whatever reason, they've drifted.

- Why don't they buy for you anymore?

- That reason might well be you.

- Have you not contacted me for some time?

- Have you forgotten they were there?

- Has the original contact moved on?

- Have you actually sent information out to them?

- But not in the form that they work out that works for them?

- Have your competitors actually moved in?

Three D businesses avoid creating these sorts of customers by continually engaging with their customers in the frequency format and channels that suit the customers. So go on, get in touch with your dormant customers, reintroduce yourself, re-engage them, get them back. It's not actually about blatantly shouting at them. It's about creating dialogue, not diatribes. And we'll explore that in a chapter coming up. So here we go. Some more questions.

- Who are your dormant customers?

- When was the last time you were in touch?

- What could you do to re-engage with them?

The ninth type of customer are the draining customers. Draining customers are the ones that are costing you money, time and resources. They're simply not profitable. Research from KPMG suggests that 50% of UK businesses can't identify their most profitable customers and products and services. Three D businesses understand where their profits come from and focus their efforts and resources accordingly. They do all they can to make things profitable and are prepared to turn non profitable work down and turn those customers down. They're not afraid to say no. It's this whole idea of choosing them or losing them.

How profit focused are you? Do you know where your profits are coming from? One of the things to think about with your customers is consider this whole concept of value for time as well as value for money. It's not about how much they spend, it's how much of your time resources are taking up to deliver this. It's all about profit, not turnover. Your challenge is to either make these customers profitable or reduce and or eliminate your reliance on them. Just a few more questions.

- Do you know who your draining customers are?

- What can you do to make them profitable?

- Should you be saying goodbye to them?

And the last type of customer is the dumped customers. These are the customers you don't want and you've consciously got rid of. That's a good thing, provided you've done it consciously and rationally. Maybe they had unrealistic, unreasonable expectations. They didn't pay you on time. They didn't pay you. What we're actually looking at is should there be more of these? As I mentioned earlier, customer focused businesses choose them or lose them and proactively develop relationships with the customers they want to work with. They're not afraid to say no.

- Should you be saying no to create more dumped customers? And no, I'm not suggesting your customers, after listening to this and just start hurling abuse at them. But can you reduce your reliance on them?

- Can you reduce your efforts and resources that you pour into them?

- Can you just say no?

- And should you encourage your people to do the same?

- So some last questions.

- What's your criteria for creating dumped customers?

- Does everybody understand this?

- Dare you and dare they dump them?

So what I'm saying, having gone through these ten types, is that maximizing customer relationships is a way of doing things. It's a philosophy. It's an attitude, and it's one that has to be shared throughout the whole of the business. So I would encourage you not to just tick a few boxes and work on this. It's actually about working out what it means for you. So create some time to work on the ten DS of customers and work out what it means for you. What's the next chapter to actually see how you can do that?

Developing Your Plan

So we've introduced you to the ten DS of different customers and the approach you need to take. Hopefully you've downloaded the toolkit if you haven't made sure you get it, because what I want to do is just take you through this and work out how to use it. So just a quick recap of the things we talked about.

Disinterested customers stay away from them. Ideal customers get more detached, Customers find ways to exceed their expectations, to create delighted customers. Do this consistently to create devoted customers, you've got to maximize them. Disappointed customers. The ones you've got to spot and deal with it. Disaffected customers show them and show others. You've done that.

Dormant customers re-engage them, get them back involved, draining customers, dump them, and dump customers. Good Keep them there. So one last question. What are you going to do? So work your way through the toolkit. I would really encourage you if you can create a bit of time and get others involved. The way I've seen this work quite well is give everybody a copy of it, get them all to do it, and then come together to create a real picture of what's happening. Remember, you might have a slightly different perspective of the people, but as a result of doing that, then prioritize your actions as a team. Develop a plan and identify the steps you need to take to create more focus on the right customers. So have a go and on 11th D do something.

Do You Really Know Your Customers?

How well do you know your customers? Do you really know them? Just look at this as an example. These are real people. If you can work out who they are to customers. Customer one Male born 1948, grew up in England. Second marriage. Two children. Successful, wealthy. Enjoys skiing in the Alps and winter. I Like dogs. Customer two Male Born in 1948.

Grew up in England. Second marriage. Four children. Successful. Wealthy. Enjoys skiing in the Alps in winter. I Like dogs. You'd think there'd be similarities, right? Similar. The demographics, as they say, are very, very clear that these are very two similar people. Any idea who those customers are? Customer one and Customer two. Well, Customer one is Prince Charles. Customer two is Ozzie Osborne. Two very different people.

And what I'm suggesting here is that we often hear marketing experts talk about segmentation, which is a way of grouping customers together and sending the appropriate messages to these groups. And traditionally, we're often told to use demographics to do this, which is finding people with similar characteristics. So age, family circumstances, income, but they often ignored things like interests, attitudes, values, all important things that influence people's needs and wants and therefore their buying behaviors.

The example we've talked about illustrates the danger of just using demographics so Prince Charles, Ozzie Osborne have similar demographics. I suspect their needs and their way to approach them might be subtly different. 3D businesses understand their customers, their needs, their aspirations and how they feel, and they use this to maximize relationships and opportunities. It can be done in lots and lots of ways. It could be something as simple as knowing your customers' key reasons for buying from you and getting to know what sort of jokes you could tell them from buying into them.

Whole idea of sophisticated big data technology, which precisely tracks customers buying habits, their patterns, what goes on, how they do things, and then responds accordingly. Think Amazon. You recently purchased this. You might like that. It's all done. Very automatic and automated whichever way you do it in order to sell more to your customers. A key factor of success is getting to know them and I mean really knowing them.

How well do you know your customers? Are you sure? What do you need to know and understand? Well, what I'm going to do is share with you a framework. As ever, there's a toolkit you can download to look at your approach to dealing with customers. And when we go through this, see if you can identify any gaps in your knowledge. I think it's important that you get a good understanding of seven key things. I'm going to take you through those seven things and give yourself some time to work out how you rate against these things. And maybe more importantly, do you actually work on what you need to do to fill the gap as we go through these?

Think about your business, think about your approach, and think about your customers. So for each of your key customers, you need to have a clear picture of the following things. One Their position in the DMU. DMU The DMU is the decision making unit. That's the people or the group of people, or sometimes the person who has influence on how to spend, when to spend, where to spend and who to spend with.

The decision making unit is actually made up of three key elements: the people, the person with the cash, the people or the person with the authority to spend that cash and the people or the person with the need for the product or service you're selling. It's the can. And one of the things that we see three D businesses do is have a clear understanding of what that looks like with the customers they're dealing with, who are the people that influence and can influence when they spend with you, how they spend with you, if they spend with you.

So some things to be aware of: who else influences the decision to use your products and services and to buy them? Who else should you be, could you be engaging with? So how aware are you of the DMU with your key customers? So let's move on to the second characteristic key factor of things that you need to know. The second one is understanding your customers aspirations, plans and needs. It's about identifying potential opportunities by developing a real understanding of where they're heading and what they're trying to achieve.

- For example, things you might want to find out what are their future plans?

- Are they growing?

- Are they developing?

- Do they like to spend more?

- What are they looking for in a supplier like you?

- Do they see the need for your products and services increasing in the future?

- How accurate can you get a picture of that as a minimum?

- Can you work out whether it's going to be increasing, decreasing, staying the same?

So again, one of the things I get you to think about is how well do you understand where your customer is heading and what they're trying to do ? Third ingredient to think a bit about and this builds on this is what are their worries and concerns? What are the things that are holding them back? 3D businesses identify the potential opportunities with existing customers by developing an understanding of the challenges and issues that they face. For example, some things to think about.

What are your customers' worries and concerns about using people like you, using other people, just maybe generally their worries and concerns?

- What's keeping them up at night?

- What's holding them back?

- What disappoints them about suppliers and businesses like you?

- Maybe what disappoints them about you again?

- How clear are you about what your customers are concerned about?

Worries are things that are actually stopping them moving forward because they could be creating opportunities for you. The fourth thing to be aware of is their expectations of you as a supplier. Establish a clear picture of how your customers view what you do for them. This could include things like what do they expect from a supplier like you? What are their priorities? How do they measure whether you're actually delivering for them? So again, are you clear about what their expectations are? And are all the people in your team clear five how well they think you're doing?

What we see 3D businesses do is establish a clear picture of how customers think they're performing. This could include things like how do they think you're doing in providing the products and services they want from you? What do you do well, What do you not do so well? How well do you satisfy and exceed their expectations? What could you do to improve an interesting one? How do you compare with your competitors? Again, how clear are you about the individual expectations of the different customers that you're serving that you're looking after? So let's move on to the next ingredient, and that is ingredient six, and that is their perception of what you can do.

This is about investigating their understanding of what products and services you offer and identify any potential opportunities or missed opportunities. For example, find out when they use you, when do they use your competition? When do they do it themselves, whether they could be using you? Are they aware of your full range of products and services? Are they using somebody else for something that you can do maybe better than them? What percentage of their spend is spent with you Again, you might need to spend some time working out and working out what these things mean for different customers.

But the more opportunities you can spot, the clearer picture you have of what they're looking for and maybe what their perception of you is, you might find that creates opportunities for you and for your business. Then let's move on to the next ingredient. And the next ingredient is actually getting to understand and know them personally. This is about building rapport.

- It's not about prying or invading their privacy, but it's understanding their personal circumstances, their interests, their aspirations. These can be a real key building block in actually developing stronger relationships. For example, with your key customers, what's their background?

- What are their ambitions?

- What do they like to do out of work?

- What's important to them at work?

- What motivates or motivates them?

- What inspires them?

- What turns them on and off Again, how well do you understand your key customers?

What makes them tick so you can actually build a better picture of what they're looking for, but also actually then start building rapport with them. So those seven characteristics, how do you measure up against those? What do you need to do to find out? Download the assessment tool, work out where your gaps are, and then work out how well you know your customers, what processes you need to have to actually get to know them and how are you going to demonstrate that you know them?

And here's a little extra question: How are you going to do it better? The next chapter actually explores some very simple processes to actually work out what you can do to get to know your customers.

How To Get To Know Them: Some Simple Steps

So one way to find out what your customers think is to. Well, guess what? Ask them. And therefore, you might want to carry out a customer attitude survey. We've had to use a toolkit to help you do this, and there are different ways you can do it. You can actually take a long time and take a whole strategic approach to do it. Or you might even want to take some time out to do some simple conversations with key customers. But first of all, let's look at the benefits of carrying out a cosmetic survey.

What are the benefits of doing it? Well, our experience working with clients and customers to do these things, some of the things they tell us they actually find helps them do. First of all, it helps you find out what your customers think. You find out what your customers want. You find out what they need. It highlights your strengths. It highlights your weaknesses or areas you need to improve on.

It can help spot opportunities, spot threats, and generate ideas. I'd also suggest it can challenge your perceptions and your opinions. It can provide you with insights into what you should change. It can also create evidence of why you need to change. If you need to persuade others in the business. If you've got feedback from customers, you can tell other people in the business. It also suggests it shows you care. But before we move on, just have a look at this. Okay. How many F's did you see? Okay, maybe we have an unfair question.

Have another look. Here we go. Okay. How many did you see? Two, three, four. You see more than five. There are actually six. Have a look. It's the F's that we miss. And very often what we see is that there are blind spots that we have. Getting feedback from your customers can help actually remove some of those blind spots and lots of us need that. So how do you go about doing it? Well, again, here is a simple process to think about. You need to apply this to how you work with your customers and how you work in your business. So a number of steps.

Step one, identify who you're going to ask. So as I said before, you could carry out a full blown customer attitude survey, but I suggest maybe just to get things started. Start with some of your key customers or maybe think about what you did in previous exercises. Create a mix of some of the ideal customers, the ones that are delighted and voted, some of the disappointed ones and maybe some of the dormant ones work out what you can do to actually engage with them and also decide what's best for your business as a starter.

Why not try with the ones that you're already doing good things with those delighted and devoted customers? You know, the ones that enjoy working with you work with those. But then having done that gives you some confidence. Build on some of the others and start developing this in other parts of the business too. Step two is to agree with your approach. Some of the ways that we've seen people do it. Clearly you could do a written survey, not necessarily filling in lots of forms, but could you do something via survey Monkey on Google forms? Some short, sharp questions just to get some conversations going.

The downside of that is you can't get people to explain what's going on, but it can be quite a way of getting lots of information from maybe a lot of people, telephone conversations, again, a bit more ability to actually create conversations with people, probably a bit deeper. Same with face to face, although clearly takes more time. Maybe some customers might find this a bit obtrusive to actually do these things. So again, find out what's best for you and your clients. One client of ours, one of the things they organize are virtual coffees and chats. They send through some vouchers to customers to get a cup of coffee and then they actually organize a time to do it.

Other things to consider are who's going to do it. Is it going to be you? Is it going to be those that deal with the particular customers? You might spread it out amongst different people. Some advantages we've actually seen is sometimes having people that maybe don't deal with those customers day to day may allow those customers to tell some of the awkward things they maybe wouldn't tell people face to face. I've also worked with lots of clients where we've actually used trainees, apprentices or getting people on board to actually make an impact on the business.

Also, I actually find lots of universities and colleges often have students marketing students prepared to get involved in projects. This is a great, manageable project to actually find people to do these things. It's a third party. You need to get them involved in it, but it's a great way of maybe trying to get some of those views from other people. So step three is to decide what to ask. Now, there's lots of questions.

We've already talked about some of these things, but here's some questions just to get you started. I'm not saying you have to use these all the time, but just to start looking at this work out what this might mean for you and your customers. Question one: Why do you buy from us? Just be careful how you ask that one. Why do you buy from us? Tends to undermine any marketing you've actually done. When do you buy from us? You can see there are follow on questions to any of these. If you get the conversations going, what one thing could we do better? And again, what we've actually found is if you actually ask them for that, what one thing rather than how can we improve?

Because they'll give you generalizations. What one thing could we do better? Question four Name one thing we do or don't do that irritates or annoys you. Question five What is the one thing we should never stop doing? And you might want to ask an extra question here. How could we do more business? Question six These are just starters. There are lots of other things you could ask, and you may need to work out what it is you want from your customers to do.

Your challenge is to use the information gathered to highlight future potential. For example, are there mismatches in terms of your actual performance, your view of it, and your customers view? Are you missing out on opportunities because your customers don't know what you can and can't do? And we're aware that they had a need for a particular product or service. Here's a quote to sort of get you to think about this. And it comes from Richard Branson.

We know the best way to drive positive change is to learn from our mistakes and hear what our customers have to say. Our companies thrive on customer feedback. It helps us innovate and disrupt and keeps us relevant. What are you going to do to actually make sure you're keeping relevant? So go on, ask some questions, engage with customers, find out what they think, and then start doing something with the information.

Establish Ties That Bind

So we've talked about folks on the right sort of customers. We've talked about getting information and ideas from them by doing feedback surveys and finding out what they need and want. As I mentioned earlier, maximizing customer relationships is not a one way relationship. It's not a passive thing. Customers need to be engaged, and that means interacting on a business and personal level and tailoring the experience specifically to each customer to help lock them in with.

We already mentioned the ties that bind. It's about letting customers recognize the personalization. The more personalized it feels, the more difficult it is for competitors to get in there. It's about creating a bond that makes it difficult for others to break into. It's not about trapping customers in because they're there. It's because they want to be. So let's look at the key ingredients of making this happen.

One. Deliver outstanding customer experiences. It's about being easy to buy from and dealing with things in the way that customers want. For others, it's a human contact, so work out what that means for them. Find ways to delight your clients and exceed their expectations. Ensure everybody recognizes their role and the place that they've actually got in making this work and make sure that the policies and processes in place to make it work. Key ingredient two is get personal.

Get to know them and demonstrate you know them. Do your communications reinforce that? Ingredient three is to create dialogue, not diatribes. Communicate with them in a way that works for them. Create conversations, ask for feedback, respond and use it. Ingredient four is to educate and add value to them. Find ways to demonstrate who you are, what you do for them, and why you're different, but also show them that you care about them as a customer and find ways of providing something extra.

So when we look at these characteristics, how do you measure up against these things in terms of what it means for you and for your customers, and maybe more importantly, work out what they mean for you? So check out the assessment tool. Are you doing these four things? And I am actually working out what they need to do. Once you have some ideas to actually work out how to do it, what's the next chapter? And we'll give you some ideas on how to do that.

Get Personal

I had an email from a company promoting their CRM software solution. It extolled the virtues of customer relationship management and explains that CRM is a business philosophy involving identifying, understanding and better providing for your customers while building a relationship with each customer to improve customer satisfaction and maximize profits. It's about understanding, anticipating and responding to customers' needs.

It goes on to say that managing the relationships with the customer a business needs to collect the right information about its customers and organize that information for proper analysis and action. It needs to keep up to date information about those customers, make it accessible to employees and provide the know-how for employees to convert that data into products that better match the customer's needs. Their product will do exactly that. Which all sounds great. Very, very much worth having.

However, the email was sent for the personal attention of Alan Hudson of Hanselmann Consultancy and Partners. A couple of points. My name is Andy Hanselman, not Alan Hudson Shulman. Our business is called Andy Hanselman Consulting, not Hanselman and Partners Consultancy. It's also addressed to Dear Sir or Madam. No thanks. I'd argue that it's 3D. UN demonstrated CRM can't remember my name. It's the same as sending emails out to people. Dear valued customer. You don't understand my name. So here are three ideas to consider to actually help you get personal. Idea one It's in the detail.

3D businesses personalize their communication with their customers in terms of format and frequency. One size fits all does not work anymore and moving to customized communications based on individual customer behavior, interests and preferences is becoming a critical factor in building and maximizing customer relationships, whether it's done with AI related technologies or simple databases. It is possible to tailor your correspondence to your customers, and you should. So what personal customer details should you have? Well, whatever you need to create meaningful relationships with them.

Here's a starter for ten for you to really just think about in terms of whether you've got this for your customers, their personal details, how they want to be addressed. Andrew Andy. Mr.Hanselman It's Andy, by the way, apart from my mum, she calls me Andrew. Their purchasing history and maybe personal notes about them are little things that you can use to demonstrate that you actually do know them and them as a business or them as a customer. Does your database have that information? Is it up to date? What do you need to clean it up? Want to ask them? Even though there are some concerns today about data privacy?

Apparently the research suggests 73% of customers are willing to share their data for a more personalized experience. That's an opportunity. In other words, if you can actually demonstrate to customers you're going to use this to tailor the experience, they'll give you the information. Another thing to consider is what is their preferred channel or method of communication? Which leads us on to the ingredient to get permission. In days gone by, marketing was all about whoever shouted the loudest and most often. Hence a strong power of TV and radio and newspaper advertising.

The bigger the budget, the bigger the chance and the better chance you had of grabbing people's attention. Although they can still be effective promotional methods, there's lots of evidence. Now the effect is declining as we become more questioning using an increasingly diverse range of media, but also finding what we want when we want it. We go and look at ourselves. Many people see advertising as intrusive and uninvited ways of coming into it get blocked out. For example, are you in the male preference system?

- So you don't get junk mail sent to you?

- Are you ex-directory to prevent cold calls?

- Do you have a spam filter on your email system to stop uninvited emails coming in?

- What about the digital TV box that helps you skip adverts?

Permission marketing is what it's all about. Customers signing up and choosing to proactively engage. Nobody's forcing you to watch this, for example. Or at least I hope they're not. Have a look. Are you guilty of forcing your message onto people who aren't or don't want to listen? Would it be better to focus on those who want to listen, who want to be engaged? In this day and age, it's clear that the quality of contacts in your database is far better than quantity. So ask your customers, Can we contact you? What's the best format and frequency we should be doing it with? And what are you interested in? Which leads us on to ingredient three. And our research indicates that a frequent comment from customer attitude surveys when we hear from clients if you don't keep us informed. You never return our calls. Or the classic one you'll never hear from me when you're chasing an invoice or chasing a bill looking for sales. And what we're saying here is about finding out what's the best way to engage with customers.

- Do they want a fortnightly call or meeting?

- Do they want things sent to them by Instagram?

- Do they want texts and emails?

- What is the best way to work for them?

- And can you agree on the parameters and then stick to them?

And one way of doing this is to use what we call CNN. Think about the messages you send out and the message you send out. There are three basic headings C critical. This is stuff that's really vital to them, could really help them solve their problems, make them feel different to them, and actually make a real difference to what they do and how they do it. It adds value and they would actually thank you for sending it. The second N is nice to know. It's things that they enjoy. It's relevant. It makes them smile.

It helps them get an understanding of who you are and what you're doing. But please don't send too much of that. The critical stuff, the important one. The third N is noise. It's all the stuff they're not interested in the irrelevant and unrequested guff. Irrelevance is defined by them, by the way, not you. So we actually worked out what CNN means for your customers. Critical will mean different things to different individuals, even within the same organization. What I'm suggesting here, if you're regularly just sending out lots, lots of noise, guess what? The critical stuff disappears. They don't see it. They don't hear it. So again, sometimes less is more.

Making sure that it's critical and nice to know, but not noise. So take some time out to identify what you and your business needs to make it and get personal.

- Is your database up to date?

- Do your messages reach your customers?

- Are they personal?

- Are they relevant?

- Are they actually received and opened and read?

- How do you know?

- What's the next chapter to?

For some ideas to find out maybe what this means for you.

Create Dialogue Not Diatribes

So many businesses believe customer communication is simply about shouting about themselves and it simply means informing or telling their customers. 3D businesses create conversations with their customers, they interact with them and they get their opinions, thoughts and ideas. It's about dialogue, not diatribes. And just here are some examples that we've seen, because clearly there are lots of ways of doing it. And I can't tell you what you should be doing.

What I can do maybe is provide you not some magic answers, but just some things. We've seen that work. So see them as a prompt to sort of stimulate some thoughts and ideas to make it work for you and then actually make sure that it actually creates some conversations with your business. So here's an example of an IT business that created conversations with its customers and quite a lot of ongoing relationships. And one of the things they talked about was how long has it been since we had some real conversations with our customers?

And what I mean by this is when you think about your customers, when was the last time you had some real conversations with them? I don't just mean about the weather or who's won the latest TV talent show, but meaningful stuff about what you're doing, how they're doing, How often do you tap into their opinions, their thoughts, their ideas? It could be something as simple as asking, what do you think about the way we supply you? What could we do better?

And one of the things you might want to think a bit about, here are some more questions you could ask to create dialogue. In my experience, lots of businesses invest lots of time, money and effort in getting customer feedback. I also think lots of businesses waste lots of time, money and effort in getting feedback. Why? Because they ask the wrong questions. They ask lots of questions, but actually listen. Or they listen to the answers and don't actually follow them up and do anything with them. So I'm all for getting customer feedback with what he talks about this thing.

It's a great source of ideas, opportunities and it demonstrates you care, provided Of course, you listen and take action. Too many businesses simply get boxes, text, go through the motions and ask customers don't make them actually feel too uncomfortable. So it's all just about ticking the boxes. And this is an example of a forward thinking business that we worked with. And we actually got talking about this and we set up a project team with some of their young graduates, trainees and apprentices to work on this to create conversations with their clients.

They called themselves the Knowing Me Knowing You Squad. And they contacted a range of clients with a mix of telephone, virtual and face to face conversations to get their thoughts using these questions. And they're not the traditional customer feedback questions you typically get asked. I'm not suggesting you ask them all, but they are a dramatic and demonstrably different way of creating some conversations and maybe just working out where the customers are coming from. A letter went out or an email went out in various guises explaining what was going on, and then these guys actually contacted customers to get some conversations going, to challenge the status quo and identify opportunities to improve.

They also created lots of ideas, suggestions and opportunities. So here you go. Here are the questions they asked. Question one: What attracted you to us? Originally, this helped get a view of how they were seen in the marketplace originally and what their clients were looking at when they first went to them. They could use this to apply to other new clients. They also then asked, Do you still see us that way? Question two What would you do if we weren't here? This was an opportunity to give an insight into the value they placed on them as a supplier. Would clients actually notice if they weren't there?

Question three What products or services do you wish we did offer? This actually highlights an opportunity for new products and services, but actually also highlighted

what clients didn't know about what they offered because some of the things they listed this supplier was already doing. Question four Can you name one particular individual who has impressed you in our business? And again, this highlighted some of their customer champions, but also some of their unsung heroes. We actually identified there was a particular individual in the accounts department that people really raved about because of the support she gave to them.

I'd also suggest if they couldn't name anybody, maybe it highlighted that work needed to be done on building the relationship with them. Question five If Carlsberg ran our business, what would it look like? You've seen the adverts, Carlsberg doesn't do this. But if they did, what would it look like? And this one really stretched people's imagination. And even though they maybe couldn't necessarily do some of these things, it did give a few ideas as to maybe what customers saw as important and let their imagination go. Question six Who can we learn from? This helped them identify who their clients saw as role models, not necessarily in the same industry, but other organizations and businesses they could actually compare themselves with.

And it pointed out a few things that weren't happening in their industry they could learn from. Question seven What would you say to someone else who asked you about us? And their responses to this were often very revealing. And it was quite interesting because this was a real thing that gave a clear understanding of what customers actually thought about them as a business. Question eight Are you completely happy with us and what we're doing? This could only be answered yes or no, and then followed up with why or why not? But it stopped.

People actually just rationalize away when people rate them out of seven. It's a very brave question to ask. What they actually found was that lots of people did say yes. The ones who said no, there were little things they could deal with. But the obvious follow up question to that is Question nine Why? Why not? What can we do? And the 10th question was, please sum us up in just three words. And what they actually did was create a world of these responses. If you're familiar with Wordles, Wordle is basically if you get lots of words going to a website called Wordle Dotcom.

Type in all the words that were delivered and presented. The more a word is actually used, the bigger it appears in the image. Very, very powerful way of getting a picture of what customers are saying and thinking about this business. You may find those weren't questions you could ask your customers, and I'm sure some of them you can't. Why not work out and find some that you can to create some conversations and create dialogue with your customers. What have you got to lose? I would argue if you don't ask them what you might have to lose are your customers.

Another way of creating conversations are competitions. Getting people to interact with you. Innocent Smoothies, I think, are a great example of an A3D business. And one of the things that they actually did was that they actually encouraged their customers to come up with a phrase or comment that could go on the bottom of their bottles. Anybody could have submitted a few words and they wanted a maximum of 40 characters via their comment chapter on their website. It went viral. They got people talking about it, and the one that got picked up got a load of freebies.

And what they talked about was the glory of their comment being up in lights. And what they actually had was on the bottom of innocent smoothies. Bottles was the one that somebody came up with as the winner was trapped in a bottle factory. Please send help. It was all done in a fun, quirky way, completely in line with the innocent way of doing things, and it created dialogue with customers. Please be aware, however, when you do want to create dialogue with customers, you want to get their thoughts and ideas.

Be careful. You may remember a few years ago the Natural Environment Research Council, where they created the name Our Ship Online poll to name the £200 million polar scientific research ship. They asked people to come up with ideas, and if you remember, the one everybody voted for was, yes, Boaty Mcboatface. So, yes, it got some publicity, but make sure it's the right sort of publicity. Another option is to create communities for conversations.

When you start looking at this, can you get groups of customers to buy into this? When I searched for baby food, the first thing I think and look for is when it comes to my baby's diet, the important things to me are these are just two of the questions people signing up for Ella's friends, which is the Club for Buyers of Baby food products, Ella's Kitchen sign up for when they actually sign up for them. It's a family for special friends. They say that you get free gifts, vouchers, newsletters, tips and advice about nutrition and weaning for your little ones. They ask for details on some simple questions to find out more about you. They actually created a community of people that they tap into.

Could you create a community of people? You could actually tap into some of your key valued customers, make them feel special, actually get them on board with these things. Another fantastic example of this is a business called John's Crazy Socks based in New York. John Lee Cronin is a truly inspirational entrepreneur. He's got Down syndrome and he co-founded with his dad, John's Crazy Socks. And guess what? Yep, they sell crazy socks. And in less than three years, I've actually built a business of over $6 million through what they call spreading happiness through socks.

And they work incredibly hard at educating their customers through ongoing interaction on their Facebook page and social networks. John's dancing videos are becoming a reputation. Everybody sort of really looks at those, and they're a regular feature of their things. They also do discussions where they actually talk about some of the things they're up to. They engage customers. They have a thing called the Sock of the Month club, their speciality gift boxes and bags. You can visit the office, you can come and see them.

We were very lucky to go and visit them a couple of years ago and they actually create a community of people who actually are bought into what they're about and it creates lots of repeat business referrals, recommendations. So I really encourage you to consider getting people to buy in to create communities formally, informally, online, offline, to engage with your customers and create dialogue. Another way of creating dialogue is feedback.

In conversations, a client of mine was dealing with Marks and Spencer's online and they sorted the issue out. There's a bit of a query, what she was doing, and she sorted it all out. When it was all finished, she actually got an email from Marks and Spencer saying, Sarah dealt with you on that. How did you rate her response? My client told me she ticked the box that said, Very good. Off it went. She got another email that said, Thanks for that. How do you think we should reward Sarah with a cup of tea, a bit of lunch or a gift card? They were actually asking her to identify what Sarah should get. As a reward and recognition for these things.

What Tony also did, she tested it. If she put zero, didn't do very well. Did it say, should we sack and watch it, but didn't actually say how can we improve? So what I'm saying here again is rather than just tick box exercises, create some conversations. When you're getting feedback from people, when you do get feedback from people for customer satisfaction, do you actually thank them for it? Some of the things to consider that I've seen work well online opinion polls again through social media just get people talking about these things. It could be things that are key in your industry.

Trends that are going on, create Facebook groups, get people engaged with what you're doing. Now, clearly, if your customers are on Facebook, but LinkedIn allows these things to create your own, bring people together to discuss key things, ask for tools and tips, get people to comment on what they've found works with working with your products and services. Simple other things. Comment on your customers' Social media. Do you have any mechanism to spot what's going on out there? Have you hashtagged?

Have you actually highlighted and alerted for some of the things that are going on with some of your customers and key customers? What I'm suggesting here is dialogue, not diatribes, is what it's about. Find ways to interact with your customers. What are you going to do to create dialogue, not diatribe with your customers? Download the assessment tool, find out how you're going to do it, and take the steps you need to actually create dialogue, not diatribes with your customers. And while you're on this one, please let us know what you think. Get in touch with us and we can actually build on this with our business too. Thank you.

Educate Your Customers And Add Value

Beth Flanagan runs an accountancy business called Mind Your Assets, and she regularly does value adding short videos, providing tips, techniques and advice to her clients via Facebook. She provides comments and help when new legislation comes out or when changes in rules and regulations are announced. She actually provides thoughts, views, ideas.

Her clients, who are mainly small entrepreneurial businesses, really value her practical and pragmatic advice. It's not up there in the middle of nowhere where we've got some blue sky thinking about accountancy. It's practical stuff that her customers can actually use, and it's just a great example of a business who is educating their customers in a way that works for them. It also reinforces her credibility, keeps her in view of her clients, and actually creates a lot of inquiries too, from non clients. I got an email from my gym.

Honestly, I do go and it highlights the peaks and troughs in terms of usage in the gym. It actually explained when they were busiest, when they weren't and was basically saying if you can come at quieter times, this might help you and it might help us by educating me about what might be best for me and maybe just getting me to question what I did and how I did it. CB Plus are an engineering business based in the Midlands, and they have actually found to actually engage with their customers. They've done some videos introducing employees and these employees explain who they are, what they do and how they do it.

They do behind the scenes videos of what's going on in the business, and it just puts a human touch to a business that works well with its customers, but actually shows who else is doing these things and actually helps people get involved in this stuff. It doesn't create lots and lots of new opportunities. What it does do is explain who they are, what they do, and maybe demonstrates that they are real people. But what they have actually found that it does every now and then is get customers to go.

We didn't realize you did that, didn't know you did that. But yeah, 52 is an online beer subscription website run by the entrepreneur Fraser Doherty. He tells a great story. Whenever they're looking to develop new ideas, they actually run it past some of their customers. They actually run virtual beer festivals where they bring people together to actually tip techniques. People can make recommendations. They actually connect their customers virtually when they start doing these things. Energy. Ian is an engineer at an air conditioning business called Air Master, and he provides online advice about heating, air conditioning and energy uses. He does online videos and blogs.

He does questions and answers. Anybody can go into their website and ask Ian. He's a great example of educating his customers. He's actually passionate about things I have no understanding of, But one of the things he actually does is he engages with customers new and old. And one of the things that these people are all doing is finding ways to add value, to educate their customers. So think a bit about what you do to educate your customers about who you are, what you do and how you do it. Some things to consider behind the scenes, videos, articles of interest or things you've actually done.

One of the things I've often seen people do is even a simple email that says, I saw this and thought of you. You could send that to lots of people. Don't do it as a mass email. So it looks as if you did make it feel personal. But one of the things that these things can actually do is highlight opportunities that you're actually creating for others that might help educate other customers. But even just simple things like new changes in legislation, let them know what's going on. Could you comment on trends in the marketplace? Give them your thoughts and views. Highlight best practice. Demonstrate how you've solved other people's problems, provide advice, anything that adds value to your customers.

But the key bit here, as ever, is in a format that works for them. Educating your customers can be done in lots and lots of ways. As ever. Think about CNN that we talked about. Is it critical? Is it nice to know? Is it noise? Think about the format. Think about the frequency, What's the best for them? And this thing about adding value, it's quite an interesting one. If you start thinking about, well, Andy, how could I add value to my customers? Well, if one of your customers was to ring you up and say, Andy, I want ten ideas how you can add value to me, to us, to our business, what would you come up with? So why not use this as a prompt to get started?

Come up with ten ideas to add value to your customers and then think about what's the best way of getting it out there. John Russell, who was the President, the European president of Harley Davidson, Europe, his quote, The more you engage with customers, the clearer things become and the easier it is to determine what you should be doing. What are you doing to engage and educate your customers to actually create the dialogue and actually make sure you're giving the best to them.

Maximize Opportunities: Your Options

So we focus so far on giving the best to your customers. We're now going to explore the whole idea of getting the best from them. And this is the payoff for all the work that you've actually done. In other words, don't just be nice to them. Let's make sure it makes commercial sense for us as a business. So what can you get from your customers?

Well, there are a number of things, and the obvious one is more sales. That would be nice, wouldn't it? Or maybe more profitable sales. You could also get commitments to longer term purchasing. You can maybe get better payment terms, but what you can also get from your customers is advice, opinions, views, ideas. Do you get referrals? Do you get them telling other people about you? Do you get testimonials? In other words, what I want you to think about when we start looking at this, getting the best from our customers, it's not just about more sales. They're great to have.

There are other options. And one of the things that we see three D businesses do is take a proactive approach to looking at these things and getting these things that they want from their customers. The next chapters will just explain step by step what those things are and how you can do it.

Getting Them To Spend More

So we're going to explore the options that you can create here for customers to spend more with you. But what are those options? Well, just think about it. There are a number of things that could possibly happen from this. There could be an increase in spending each time they purchase. So is that them spending more on the products and services you're actually offering? Is it more of the same products or services? Could it be?

Should it be different, maybe more profitable products or services? Could there be additional products and services? Could there be some new products and services? So when you start looking at this, when it looks at how you actually increase the value of the sale, have you explored the options that customers could actually be spending more with you every time they purchase from you? What they could also do is look at the increased frequency of their purchasing. How often do they spend time with you? What are you doing to engage them, to bring them back, to let them know what you're doing? And one of the ways of looking at this is a little model that we talk about called the share of customers.

And what we do with this share of the customer model. And again, you'll see a picture of it here is that the whole idea of this is that you can look at your customers on two fronts. One is high spend, one is low, spend, high spend is how much do they spend a year on the sorts of products and services that you provide? High spend, low spend. That's a very subjective thing.

You need to work out what that is. What you'll also see across here is a high share. Low share, High share is they spend a lot of their money with you. Low share is they spend it elsewhere.

And you can suddenly start looking at your customers from different perspectives. So high spend, high share. By definition, these are your key customers. You've got to stay very close to them. They're the ones you really need to know about what's going on, what their buying patterns are, what their aspirations are, what their plans are. So key customers, if there's one thing you take from this, is those are the ones I would argue you should be applying this stuff to if you're not doing it already. Low spend, high share. These are the customers you need to keep in touch with. They don't spend very often, but when they do, they come to you.

- What are you doing to keep in touch with them?

- What are you doing to educate them?

- Could you get that expense up?

- Or as a minimum, could you make sure that you remind them that you're there?

Please, Whatever you do, don't put too much time into those at the cost of your key customers. Low spend, low share, keep out, don't bother with. But this is an interesting one. High spend, low share. They spend a lot each year on the sorts of products and services you're providing, but they're not spending out with you.

- Why?

- Why is that?

- Why do you think somebody could be in that box?

Maybe it's because they're not aware of the products and services you provide. Maybe it's because you're not spending enough time with them because you've not been doing the things we've been talking about. Maybe they are in habits. They spend this with you, they spend that with them. Maybe they have a policy that doesn't allow them to spend more with a certain percentage with a particular supplier, at least if you know that, that's fine. But are there opportunities there with existing customers that are actually you could focus on and you could work on?

In other words, these customers in this box are maybe the opportunities for you to build on this stuff and make it work. You might have identified some of these with your cosmetics surveys we've talked about in the past. If you've not done it yet, this again might help you decide that it's a thing to do. So again, what we suggest you do is download the template with this, get your team together and actually work out where your customers are.

Very often when I do this, I get sales teams together and guess what I say, where would you put the different customers? And they're all different individuals, put the same customers in different boxes because they don't know. Another engineering business that I worked with, one of the things that they did, they actually identified who these customers were and recognized that they were buying certain products and services and not others. So they decided to go on a proactive approach to what they called tell and sell.

And each of the sales account managers were given their customers and they identified first of all of their customers which of them were buying and using which products and services. So they actually identified where the gaps were, and they were all tasked with educating, explaining to their customers for the next couple of months and telling them about the different products and services they're doing, which wasn't forcing them to do things. It was about asking the questions, doing something as we've talked about, But they proactively did it and reported back each month and there was a little grid where they could actually show that they told the customer.

They ticked the box if they'd sold to them, they filled the box in. But what I'm suggesting here is if you could start targeting your customers at certain customers who aren't aware of some of the products and services you provide, tell them. Explain it with some of the ways we've talked about today. But then key importantly, work on what you need to do to actually sell them to them. What we actually found, this actually created a real focus for the team and actually helped them maximize opportunities by not just giving the best to, but getting the best from the customers with increased sales of new products and services that lots of their customers didn't know they provided. So work out what this means for you to actually educate your customers and let them know what it is you're doing to actually get them to spend more. That's this whole idea of getting the best from your customers when it comes to sales.

Customers As An Extra Resource

So hopefully I've already highlighted the benefits of getting feedback from customers on what you do and how you do it. Well, one of the things you can actually maybe do is look at how you build on that. So one of the ways of getting the best from customers yet is to sell more to them, but it's also about getting their thoughts and ideas. So why not consider involving them in developing new products or services?

Test it on them, get feedback on it, involve them, make them feel special. In other words, ask your customers to actually give them your thoughts and views on what they think about this new product or service. Tom Bloomfield, the founder of Monzo Bank, a quote that I love from him. We believe the best way to build a great product is by launching it early and improving it based on feedback from real people. I am very lucky that we have a community of users that care enough to share their enthusiasm, ideas and frank feedback with us.

They've helped us make Monzo what it is today, and I'm glad that so many people have chosen to join us for that, for what's next. In other words, what he's actually doing there, if they've got a new product or service, they test out customers. If you've created that community of people that we talked about earlier, they might be the ones doing this. And I was at an event where he was speaking where one of the things that Monzo does is that they're a challenger bank, if you don't know who they are originally targeted at, young professionals.

And one of the key benefits that they offered people was that you can actually withdraw money abroad for free up to £200. But what they actually found was that quite a few of their customers were maybe young people traveling and what they would do is they'd just draw €20 a day, €30, €20, €10 each day. What Monzo had to explain to their customers was that because of the whole way the network banks worked, the big banks in Europe would charge Monzo for every transaction. So Monzo actually emailed their customers and said, If you can.

You don't have to. But if you could, could you try and do this maybe just once a month? Because it's costing us as a business. Over 90% of customers responded and did that. I suspect if you were to get an email from maybe some of the more traditional banks in this country and ask them to actually say, please don't do this, I'm not sure they'd get that sort of response. In other words, you've got here is a business who's built its relationships with its customers to get on board with these things. Test ideas. I mentioned before Fraser Doherty of Bay 52, they've created this community of users. They actually call them the beer friends. And what they do is they actively get people to sign up and they actually get involved with providing feedback. So you actually become part of the community.

You actually sign up for that. But also think about reviews. Do you get feedback from customers? Do you ever get your customers to actually put reviews on trustpilot on Google reviews? Maybe encourage them, ask them to do it. I'm not asking you to force them to write things they shouldn't be doing. What I'm getting them to do here is just say please, please, please give us a review. Make it easy for them to do it.

And again, please thank them for doing it. Thank them for giving you the feedback, comment on it.

Show to them that you've actually listened to them and you actually see what they're doing. Ask for testimonials. If you're asking customers about how good you are and they say you're doing a great job. Ask for a written testimonial. Maybe even better. Can you get a video? One doesn't have to be super sexy. It's going to be functional. But make sure that it actually demonstrates who you are and what you're doing. Build it into your feedback processes. Thank your customers for doing this. You could even consider incentivizing them to do it. And in my experience with this is that most customers, if they've had a great bit of feedback from you, for you, they'll actually tell you people, but make it easy for them to do it and referrals ask for them.

Maybe build it into your feedback process. You might remember I mentioned earlier the business that had known me, knowing you crew that were going out, asking customers about would you refer us? They actually then said, if you could refer us, who would you refer us to? They were amazed how many people actually said, I need to talk to this person, and they actually gave it to them. And then what I'm suggesting here again is have you built into your feedback processes, ways to create and generate referrals within the organizations and customers or elsewhere?

Have a go at it and work on this. A fantastic organization has really tapped into doing this and getting their customers to spread the news for them is an organization called Charity

Water. This is an international charity that actually provides fresh water to impoverished areas around the world, and one of the things they set up a thing to do was to leverage their relationships by a little thing called the birth initiative. And they actually encouraged their donors, some of their customers, some of their fans to actually say to their family and friends, rather than give me a birthday present this year, if I'm a 20 year old, please just give me £20.

And what they actually then would do, they'd get seven year olds getting $7. They were six year olds getting $60, £60. It's a great little way. They make it easy to do it. You do a little video, you tell people about it. But guess what? It spreads. The word, people go, That's a good idea. I'll try that. Well, last year they raised over $9 million doing that. And what they actually find is that the average birthday pledge is around $770 and they help on average, 38 people are getting gauged each time. So they've got the numbers to tell them what's going on, which is a good sign.

But it's also a fantastic way of getting other people to talk about their organization. And I would encourage you to have a look at Charity Water. It's a fantastic 3D organization. Have a look at what they're doing. They're doing some brilliant stuff. Again, it's that word of mouth thing working again there. But work out what you need to do to leverage your relationships with your customers. Find out what they can do to help you. And a little appeal. If you found this program or any of the programs on Expert Academy work, please tell other people. Again, that's us practicing what we preach.

Maximizing Your Customer Relationships: Develop Your Plan

So let's summarize what we've talked about. Forget CRM, think mixer. Maximizing customer relationships is definitely not about heavy sales pusher selling techniques. It's about proactively developing relationships that give the best to and get the best from the customers you want. How can you do that?

Well, the key factor for success that we've talked about is those three D businesses. One. Think strategically and get focused. That's a strategic view. And create win-win relationships with customers they want to do that with. They ensure their efforts and resources are focused on customers they want to prioritize and they actually make sure this is happening. Key Success Factor two.

They understand what their customers think and want. They understand who their best customers are, what they want from them, and what a maximizing relationship looks like. What they do is they get to know them. They carry out attitude surveys. They create conversations with them to find out what they need and want and then tailor their offer to each of those customers, which is demonstrated in key Factor three. They get personal. They make their customers feel valued by personalizing their offer and the communication and the way they do it. It could be the frequency. It could be the format. It could be the messages. But they make sure that customers feel it's been personalized to actually create those ties that bind.

Key Success Factor four. They create dialogue, not diatribes. They listen to their customers. They recognize that their customers need to be engaged.

Result Find ways of creating conversations online, offline, the appropriate channels for the customers in the frequency and format the customers actually want. They get mechanisms in place to get customer feedback and tell their customers what's really going on out there to actually help them do that. By. Five Success Factor five Add value. They regularly and proactively provide customers with relevant new ideas and solutions that add value. They don't shout at them. They do things that take away the pain to solve problems, to educate their customers, but they do it in an appropriate and timely manner that works for the customer, not just themselves, but that allows them for key ingredient six to maximize opportunities and think share of customer as well as giving the best to their customers.

They also focus on getting the best from them, usually in the form of repeat business, more opportunities and loyalty. They also ensure that their people can spot and maximize other opportunities to make it work for them. In simple terms, maximizing opportunities is the payoff is an integral part of maximizing customer relationships. They proactively identify where those opportunities exist. They educate their customers about their total capabilities and work out what it means for them to proactively build and maximize their relationships. And key success.

Factor seven is they leverage the relationships. They get their customers to give back. That could be in terms of feedback, ideas, suggestions, testimonials, recommendations and referrals. They proactively encourage and maybe incentivize their customers to do that. So download the assessment tool again, work out how your business measures up. You might have scored this earlier. I'd encourage you to do it again because it could be that after the Book you start to realize that maybe you're not as good as you thought. Work on the areas you've got to work on and develop your own plan of action. Involve others and make it work for you.

I'm going to finish off with a quote from Seth Godin, the marketing guru. Selling to people who actually want to hear from you is more effective than interrupting strangers who don't. What are you doing to sell to people who actually want to hear from you and maximize those customer relationships? So consider your next steps. Work out what it is you're going to do. Use the toolkit, use the template, but also just watch the final chapter just to get a quick insight into what you can do next and maybe how we can help you do it. Have a look. All the best with it.

Your Next Steps

Hopefully now you are maximizing your customer relationships. I just thought I'd highlight that there are other Books on the Expert Academy that you can access and used to actually build on these things. We've got Books on three D leadership and we've got Books on how three D businesses perform on things like leadership. There's a Book on leadership, how to actually create strategic focus and make your business work.

We've actually got a Book on employee engagement, how to get people on board, get the best out of your people. There's a Book on culture on how to create a culture that supports all these things. We've got one on marketing, how to create and find customers that come to you. And we've also got one that looks at creating outstanding customer experiences. Some things we've talked about today: How can you make this work or practical, pragmatic things you can do to help you become A3D business and A3D leader? So please get in touch with any questions, queries and successes you've had.

You can get in touch with me via Andy hanselman.com and I can engage with you on LinkedIn. On Facebook, on Twitter. I'd love to know how you've got on. Please let us know. All the best. Take care.